Black Dignity

BLACK DIGNITY

THE STRUGGLE
AGAINST DOMINATION

● ● ●

VINCENT W. LLOYD

Yale

UNIVERSITY PRESS

New Haven and London

Published with assistance from the Mary Cady Tew Memorial Fund.

Yale University Press books may be purchased in quantity for
educational, business, or promotional use. For information, please e-mail
sales.press@yale.edu (U.S. office) or sales@yaleup.co.uk (U.K. office).

Excerpted pages 2, 6, 7, 8, 9, 17–18, 19, 22, and 51 from *Notebook of a
Return to a Native Land* by Aimé Césaire. Copyright © 2001 by Clayton
Eshleman and Annette Smith, trans. and ed. Used by permission of
Wesleyan University Press.

Set in Gotham and Adobe Garamond type by IDS Infotech Ltd.,
Chandigarh, India.
Printed in the United States of America.

Library of Congress Control Number: 2022938399
ISBN 978-0-300-25367-2 (hardcover : alk. paper)

A catalogue record for this book is available from the British Library.

This paper meets the requirements of ANSI/NISO Z39.48-1992
(Permanence of Paper).

10 9 8 7 6 5 4 3 2 1

Contents

Preface   vii

1   Everything Black   1
2   Black Rage   38
3   Black Love   56
4   Black Family   74
5   Black Futures   93
6   Black Magic   112
7   I Believe in the Revolution   131
   Afterword: How to Live with Dignity   153

Notes   165
Acknowledgments   181
Index   183

Preface

In August 2018, I found myself returning a rental car in Florissant, Missouri, the St. Louis suburb next to Ferguson. I had driven fourteen hours from my home in Philadelphia with my suitcases and pit bull to spend a year near the neighborhood that had become a symbol of Black protest. Just a few years before, I had been convinced that Black politics was over, the struggle for racial justice abandoned. The era of the struggle's great heroes, Frederick Douglass, W. E. B. Du Bois, Ida B. Wells, and Anna Julia Cooper, had passed. Martin Luther King, Jr., was now an icon of peace, love, and nonviolence celebrated by all. The Black leaders who occupied the media spotlight were either caricatures of King, clinging to his memory, or else they accepted the terms of electoral politics, naming diversity as one issue among many on which work remained to be done. A few intellectuals spoke out about systemic racism; a few radicals organized Black folks for occasional protests. But the grandeur of the Black political tradition, the way it tightly tied together a deep-cutting critique to the slow grassroots work of organizing, was a thing of the past.

Then a police officer shot at a Black teenager named Michael Brown twelve times and let his body lie on a Ferguson street for four hours. Local Black youths took to the streets to protest, the police responded with armored cars and tear gas, and the national spotlight shone on Ferguson to uncover what Black folks there knew all too well: that they were chronically subject to exorbitant city fines, police harassment, and police violence. Black Americans across the country recognized the violence to body and soul on display in Ferguson as the same violence we faced daily in our communities. The political environment was shifting, but so was the political vocabulary employed by Black youths and young adults who identified with the struggle. Where diversity, multiculturalism, racism, and nonviolence had been the language of African American politics, a new era of capital-B Black politics was opening, with a new moral vocabulary. The hashtag Black Lives Matter came to name the movement, but the movement is also defined by Black rage, Black love, Black family, Black futures, Black study, and Black girl magic, among others.

Over the course of my year in Missouri, I talked with Black youths who had been involved in the Ferguson uprising and with middle-class Black folks who observed it. I returned to the Black classics with new eyes. I began to understand that the hashtags circulating in Ferguson and around the Black world formed a coherent moral-political vision. The thread running through that vision, orienting it toward struggle, is a commitment to Black dignity.

In this book, I sketch out the vision of today's racial justice movement. I also think with that vision, probe it, and give it shape and coherence that I did not find in the words of movement participants, even as I take those words as a starting point. Put another way, this is not a traditional work of philosophy that sets out axioms and works from premises to conclusions. Instead, I move back and forth between listening and structuring, between activist rhetoric and crisper, connected concepts. While this may frustrate readers looking only for a description of activist beliefs or for a systematic theory of dignity, I believe my method is the best way to take activists seriously, as intellectuals whose thought grows out of and refines through the struggle for justice.

Taking activists seriously also means, at times, disagreeing with them. Professed commitments do not always match an underlying orientation, especially in the heat of protest. I am interested in the deeper currents of struggle, which I believe continue and strengthen the tradition of Black struggle that has run for decades and centuries. Unfortunately, we live in a moment when disagreement on matters associated with race stops conversations, when precise affirmation (or retweeting) of a certain discourse on race cleaves friends from enemies. We are stuck at the surface, in the moment. I take risks to dive deeper: challenging the conventional wisdom of public discourse and movement discourse, turning not only to revered Black leaders of the past but also to those overlooked or dismissed as suspect, and making arguments about how best to live and to struggle that are not perfectly aligned with activists, although I believe we are motivated by the same imperatives. This is philosophy: asking tough questions that push beyond platitudes. You may disagree on this point or that, but I invite you into the rough-and-tumble of ideas, guided by the call of justice.

My trip to Missouri was not the first time I left home searching for the meaning of Blackness. A dozen years earlier I took two suitcases filled with my earthly belongings and flew to South Africa. Then I had even less sense of what I was looking for; perhaps, just a decade after the end of apartheid, I imagined I would find Black people more attuned to struggle. Instead I found Black elites basking in their newfound wealth and status. I befriended Zimbabwean refugees and organized with them against xenophobia. I read and wrote: in Johannesburg I escaped into European philosophy and drafted my first book, on the philosophical desire for transcendence, in the evenings after fixing myself a potful of pap in my room.

For many years, wherever I lived, this was my life: writing and teaching by day, organizing by night, or vice versa. I organized with undocumented workers in New York, with unionized service workers in New Jersey, with senior citizens fighting gentrifying efforts to close their senior center, with students fighting cutbacks in public education. I read and wrote about Hegel and Nietzsche, Foucault and Derrida, Levinas and Badiou. I was escaping my Blackness, but also looking for my Blackness. I wrote about how the desire for transcendence is nearly unavoidable and almost always goes wrong; I worked with communities struggling, almost always in vain, to transcend the domination they faced. The condition of the world, I concluded, is tragedy. Our dissatisfaction fuels us forward, offering faith without hope. When we imagine transcending our circumstances, we are led astray, but our impulse to engage with the world throws us into failure after failure.

As a millennial, I came of age during the heyday of multiculturalism. We learned to celebrate diversity. Instead of just Christmas cookies, our winter project in kindergarten included recipes for Hanukkah cookies, Diwali cookies, and Kwanzaa cookies. But for me, as a Black boy growing up in Minnesota, multiculturalism took away my ability to talk about myself. It told a happy story; I knew it to be a lie but could not explain why. I was filled with unease, and I worked this unease by looking elsewhere. I challenged the comforting stories philosophers told about transcending difference, and I organized with non-Black communities to attack domination.

It takes fourteen hours to drive from Philadelphia to St. Louis; I did it alone, stopping only to buy gas and to eat. As I drove out of Philadelphia, through the suburbs, past the mountains of Pennsylvania and the plains of Ohio and Indiana, as I crossed the Mississippi, sighted the signs for St. Louis, and finally pulled into the parking lot of the Florissant Hertz, I remembered moments from my life that I had forgotten, that multiculturalism had made illegible. I remembered being stopped by police on my way to the public library one summer day because they were looking for a suspect with "dark hair." I remembered the boy at summer camp who told me each day that Blacks were unwelcome, and punctuated his point on the last night by bashing my head into a bunk bed frame. I remembered a police officer approaching me when I was studying one evening in a college common room, asking for an ID that I didn't have on me, and then escorting me out of the building. I remembered a landlord calling my girlfriend's mother to ask if she knew her daughter was living with a Black man. I remembered being attacked on the street by a group of Black teenagers one evening on the South Side of Chicago. When the police showed up, they looked warily at me, still crumpled on the ground, until I showed them my University of Chicago ID card. Then they were eager to help and wanted to know what I could remember. The only thing I remembered—imagined—the boys saying was that I was white.

The new moral vocabulary I found near Ferguson allowed me to put my Blackness into words and gave me a way to understand the depths of anti-Blackness shading America. Anti-Black racism is not just about bad choices, or about people who failed their diversity exam. It is at the center of everything, for everyone. It leads to police violence but also to odd looks from colleagues; it leads to mass incarceration but also makes Black bodies especially vulnerable to disease. And it makes Black people confused about who we are. All of this grows out of the primal scene of slavery.

Anti-Blackness is not a discrete set of habits and practices. It interlocks with other systems of domination: patriarchy, xenophobia, homophobia, ableism. After Ferguson, activists were increasingly talking about these connections, using them to expand the movement's vocabulary, but the discourse was messy and sometimes confused. I set out to get a sense of this new language of Black dignity, to explore how the hashtags could be filled out, linked together, and oriented toward the struggle against domination in general and anti-Blackness in particular. In the process, I was giving myself a language to understand my Blackness.

Where once I found the desire for transcendence titillating but ultimately misguided, I now realize why that desire should not be considered in the abstract. It derives from the primal scene of domination: the slave's desire to escape her master. And I see how that struggle against domination, made vivid when I imagined a slave, was the same struggle I had engaged in with undocumented workers, students seeking a decent, affordable education, senior citizens seeking to preserve their community center, and Zimbabwean refugees seeking acceptance in Johannesburg.

I had been looking to escape, to travel over a country or an ocean, into abstract philosophy or other communities' struggles, to find myself. Around Ferguson I finally found a language that was mine, and I also found a tradition. As I reread the Black classics, I was amazed to find how directly they spoke to me—how persistent is the anti-Blackness they name. With Bigger Thomas, I have said the twenty-first-century equivalents of yes, sir and no, sir, eliciting from whites a satisfied smile. With Celie from *The Color Purple,* I have seen the selfless acts of Black women and wondered whether they were accompanied by feelings of love or by numbness. A white professor of mine, like Audre Lorde's neighbor in *Zami,* announced that he only realized I was Black after I was a finalist for a minority fellowship. A white woman asked me to call her names, choke her, and faux-rape her, like Ralph Ellison's Invisible Man. Beyond the specifics, the feelings that pervade the Black classics, the anger, frustration, and helplessness, love, care, and joy, all mixed together and made beautiful, gave me a way to connect my passions with reason, joined together by the struggle against domination.

After I began writing this book, a white Minneapolis police officer pressed his knee into the neck of George Floyd, a middle-aged Black father, until he suffocated and died. Protesters set a Minneapolis police station ablaze. A CNN crew was arrested while broadcasting live from the protests. Unrest spread nationwide. The Black poet Aimé Césaire, after studying in Paris and meeting Black youths from around the world, concluded that "the only thing in the world worth beginning" is "the end of the world." In the streets of America today, Black youths are also calling for an end of the world, for a new world free of domination. I do not know if it will come today. But I know that today, as yesterday and tomorrow, Black people struggle, and this struggle is our dignity.

BLACK DIGNITY

1

Everything Black

The concept of dignity has long been at the center of Black politics and life. When Martin Luther King, Jr., accepted the Nobel Peace Prize, he described the civil rights movement as an attempt "to find a new sense of dignity." Stokely Carmichael spoke of assembling a coalition of Black power advocates joined by their commitment "to rebuild their dignity." Barack Obama, receiving his own Nobel, argued that "we can admit the intractability of deprivation, and still strive for dignity." From Marcus Garvey to Malcolm X, from Ida B. Wells to Angela Davis, dignity is always found around Black struggle. It is no surprise that the word shows up in the first line of the Movement for Black Lives platform, and in the way movement leaders speak of their intentions. Alicia Garza describes the movement's core commitment: "When we say Black Lives Matter, we are talking about the ways in which Black people are deprived of our basic human rights and dignity." Patrisse Cullors, who named the grassroots organization she founded Dignity and Power Now, reflects, "I come at all my work from a deep philosophical place that [asks], what does it take for humans to live in our full humanity and allow for others to live in their full dignity?" Opal Tometi, the third of the three women who put #BlackLivesMatter in circulation, says its central goal is "ensuring that all people of African descent are treated with the dignity and respect that we deserve."[1]

While the term *dignity* appears often in the history of Black politics, it has been used in such varied ways that it is not clear whether it has meaning beyond its rhetorical force. Sometimes it seems *dignity* is used as a synonym for *humanity*: to treat someone with dignity is to treat them as a fellow human, worthy of respect. Or, in a theological register, recognizing and revering the image of God in a human. But this sense of dignity as a status captures only one of its aspects; it is like the projection of a three-dimensional shape onto a two-dimensional surface. Dignity is also something you *do*, a practice, a performance, a way of engaging with the world. This is a special insight of the Black political tradition, skeptical as it is of abstractions: with time frozen, dignity may look like a status, but in its natural habitat, dignity names friction. In a world that denies Black humanity and embraces racial domination, dignity names an affirmation of that humanity, which necessarily means struggle against domination.

This more complex sense of dignity is evident when we consider the case of Black athlete, singer, lawyer, and activist Paul Robeson. When Robeson wore his legal hat—for example, petitioning the United Nations in 1951 to address racism in the United States—he invoked dignity as a status. The text of the petition enumerates "crimes inflicted on our dignity," matching the language of the emerging international human rights regime. Yet even this legal document contains hints that dignity has another dimension. The next line is "We struggle for deliverance, not without pride in our valor." One sense of dignity is attacked by racism, but this makes another sense of dignity come to light: dignity achieved in struggle, not at the end point but in the very process. This is not a concept Robeson learned from the United Nations. He spoke of dignity frequently throughout his life, as early as his 1919 valedictory address at Rutgers, through his travels in solidarity with working-class people around the world, and during his years of isolation in the United States due to blacklisting. Throughout his life, status did not exhaust the meaning Robeson found in dignity. For example, speaking about the evils of segregation in New Orleans in 1942, he proclaims, "I had never put a correct evaluation on the dignity and courage of my people of the deep South until I began to come South myself." He continues, "I see them now courageous and possessors of a profound and instinctive dignity." The dignity he invokes is the practice of living in a world bent on the destruction of Black life. Sometimes dignity connotes struggle on a grand scale, in activism and organizing; at other times the struggle is simply for survival. In either case, when the focus is on any given slice of time, dignity has the appearance of a status possessed; such a focus ignores the richer sense of dignity in motion.[2]

As a singer and actor, Robeson was frequently described as a paradigm of dignity: dignity practiced, performed. In his portrayals of working-class people throughout the world, from Welsh miners to Jewish resistance fighters to Black Americans, he translated the struggles he encountered into stories and songs with which all could identify. In his own performances, Robeson made visible the dignity of those struggling against the denial of their humanity—making dignity contagious. As actor and activist Ossie Davis said of Robeson, "We have no category, even now, to hold the size of him. Something about him escapes our widest, most comprehensive embrace." Black studies scholar Shana Redmond titled her recent study of Robeson *Everything Man*. But the expansiveness he embodied had its origins in the very particular experience of slavery. While Robeson was a paradigm of dignity for many audiences, his own paradigm of dignity was his father, who had been born in slavery and would later become a Presbyterian minister. From his father, Robeson learned "that a so-called lowly station in life was no bar to a man's assertion of his full human dignity." The elder Robeson did not avert his eyes or bow down to whites, his body itself asserting dignity. In short, for Robeson, dignity is performed in multiple registers, political, everyday, aesthetic, and bodily, always in struggle, and ultimately routed through the experience of slavery.[3]

Note how Robeson invokes dignity to name the struggle against inhumanity, against the denial of dignity as status. This is key to dignity in Black thought: Black writers repeatedly distinguish between dignity in a stale, hollow sense and in the full, true sense. Those who are ascribed the status of dignity often do not really have it in the robust sense; those who are denied the status of dignity often do really have dignity. In "August 19th," a poem written in 1938 about the Black teenagers, known as the Scottsboro Boys, wrongly accused of raping white women in Alabama, Langston Hughes writes, "A young black boy will die" yet "Judges in high places / Still preserve their dignity." Those judges seem to have dignity but do not. They are but cogs in the machine of white supremacy, and in service to that machine they have become child-killers. A decade later, in "Harlem Dance Hall," Hughes depicts dignity at its fullest. The poem begins and ends by proclaiming that the hall "had no dignity before"—but when the band begins playing,

> Suddenly the earth was there,
> And flowers,
> Trees,
> And air.

Dignity is realized in performance rather than in status, in dancing rather than in sitting, in harmony with nature rather than in being elevated above the world. An empty building lacks dignity; dignity is to be found in bodies moving in rhythm. This might not seem like an especially political or moral idea of dignity. But Black folks gathering in a world that would keep them apart, Black folks moving in a world that would keep them still, Black folks aligned with nature in a world that makes their lives unnatural—these are forms of struggle. They are challenges to those who would deny dignity to Blacks. Black dignity pushes against this denial; it does not enjoy a status that has been granted but claims a status that has been denied.[4]

An important innovation embraced by the Black Lives Matter movement has been to cleave dignity from respectability, calling attention to the difference between a full understanding of dignity and a flat understanding that is not really dignity at all. Ordinary language often treats "dignity" and "respectability" as interchangeable, yet from the movement perspective, dignity is laudable, respectability indictable. The latter connotes an attempt to perform to a white audience, fulfilling white fantasies of how "good" Black people look and act—"clean and articulate," to borrow the words Joseph Biden used to describe then-candidate Barack Obama: well-dressed, heterosexual, middle class, deferential, knowing their place. Respectability is the illusion of dignity. This critical tool, of cleaving dignity from its false copies, is the start of explicating the philosophy of Black dignity. As the French-Algerian activist Houria Bouteldja puts it in a book inspired by the Black political tradition, "Dignity is in our ability to distinguish stars from sequins. All this artifice that white people saddle themselves with to maintain a distance and subjugate us."[5]

When we turn from dignity as status to dignity as performance, as struggle, we find it easier to state clearly what dignity is not than what it is. When Hughes tries to speak affirmatively about what Black dignity looks and feels like, he points to dancing bodies and uses metaphors. Those bodies are like the fullness of nature. This is precisely the style of analysis Black dignity requires. We cannot state necessary and sufficient conditions. We cannot offer a comprehensive list of exemplars. We cannot simply rely on knowing it when we see it. What we can do is twofold. First, we can clearly and forcefully name what dignity is not. Second, we can point to examples of where dignity could be—examples that are often fleeting performances, impossible to systematize and describable only by metaphor or in an aesthetic or imaginative register. This is the asymmetric style of analysis made necessary by the nature of dignity itself, but it is also the characteristic method of the broader philosophical project implicit in today's Black political movements that I abbreviate with the phrase *Black dignity.* We can have clarity and precision when speaking in the negative, and we appeal to the aesthetic or imaginative register when speaking in the positive. What do we want? An end to these injustices. What does justice look like? Nothing that can be captured in a systematic theory. The word *justice* is a placeholder for the inexpressible, an occasion to imagine (or dance, or sing) the world free of domination.

Frederick Douglass's eloquent narratives form the cornerstone of Black thought. The towering Black intellectual of the nineteenth century, over his life Douglass journeyed from slavery in Maryland to freedom in Massachusetts, from chattel to respected orator and writer and, finally, ambassador to Haiti. He tells in graphic detail of the horrors of slavery and relates how he came to navigate life enslaved, how he learned to read despite his owners' opposition, and how he eventually escaped. But the centerpiece of his narrative, the "turning-point," as he calls it, is his fight with the slave-breaker Covey. It is there that we find Black dignity in its purest form, in laboratory conditions, as it were.[6]

As a boy of sixteen, Douglass finds himself lent to a poor white farmer, Edward Covey, who has a reputation for crushing the will of slaves, making them pliable upon return to their owners. Covey whips Douglass repeatedly and mercilessly until Douglass runs off to his old master to appeal for help—only to be sent back to Covey. Upon his return, Covey first seems to ignore the boy's transgression. Then, as Douglass is going about his regular morning routine, feeding the horses, Covey sneaks up on him and tries to tie his legs with rope. Douglass leaps away. He has always been told to obey his master, to endure the brutality; there is no alternative. A slave who fought back could be hanged by the town constable, likely after being tortured to set an example for others who might fight back. But for reasons he himself does not understand, Douglass resolves to fight. "I found my strong fingers firmly attached to the throat of the tyrant," Douglass writes, "as if we stood as equals before the law." Douglass sees a different reality, a future where there is equality instead of domination, and animated by that vision, he is able to fight.[7]

Covey, surprised by the boy's resistance, soon realizes that, man on man, he cannot defeat or capture Douglass. The master alone cannot control the slave. He calls his cousin to aid him, but together they fare no better than Covey alone. Used to always having his way, Covey is taken aback, scared, and mute. The master lives under the illusion that he is in control, that his power to command is a natural part of who he is. When that lie is exposed, he is shaken to the bone. He appeals for more help, trying to enlist two other slaves to capture Douglass. Risking violence to their own bodies, both refuse Covey's order. After two hours of trying to capture Douglass, Covey relents. He tells Douglass to continue with the farm chores, and Douglass does—but he is now a new man. Covey will not whip him again, but there is a more significant change. The fight "rekindled in my breast the smoldering embers of liberty." Douglass was not free, but in his bodily struggle with Covey, he had a foretaste of freedom. He began dreaming more often about life without a master. At the same time, Douglass's self-image transformed: "I was nothing before; I was a man now." He had believed what his master and his world said about him, that he was less than human, just another beast of burden on the farm. Struggle inspired him to struggle again, in new ways, for his freedom. Douglass concludes, "A man without force is without the essential dignity of humanity." Dignity in struggle.[8]

Douglass acknowledges that his reader may have difficulty understanding this transformation. He suggests two tools for comprehension.

First, reflect on some time when you were involved in "repelling the unjust and cruel aggressions of a tyrant." Unspoken here is that we can all recall times in our own lives and the lives of those around us when, whether on a grand scale or, more likely, a very small one, we struggled against domination. Reflecting on those struggles, and how they transformed us, can give us a taste of what happened to Douglass: struggles against domination all have the same quality, he seems to be saying, even if they differ in intensity. Second, Douglass draws on the Christian imagination. Through struggle, he achieved new life. "It was a resurrection from the dark and pestiferous tomb of slavery, to the heaven of comparative freedom." He had been entombed, his body alive but his soul dead, crushed by his master's domination, which was enforced by an entire system of domination. With a taste of freedom, Douglass was able to participate, partially and imperfectly, in new life—life beyond domination. Moreover, the fear of death no longer had a hold on him. Compared to the struggle for freedom, death mattered little. Unafraid to die, he was "a freeman in fact, though I still remained a slave in form." The system of domination persists and controls his world, even after this crucial turning point in his life. But this matters little, as one of its prime tools, fear of death, has been dismantled. Through struggle, supported by his community of fellow slaves, Douglass begins to manifest in the present the future freedom he desires.[9]

In short, *dignity means struggle against domination.* The more struggle, the more dignity; the less struggle, the less dignity. The judges in the Scottsboro case have no dignity, only a false copy of dignity, because they do not struggle at all. They allow the system to work smoothly and are no more than properly functioning components of it—a system of racial domination. At their core, those judges are undignified. Dignity is found where there is friction, where someone does not play her part. Dignity does not have to look like a political protest, though it can; it can also look like song, dance, jokes, sermons, or silence. In each case, dignity names performance, activity (including the activity of refusal), rather than result. Even in the specifically political case, dignity is not the status achieved; it lives in the process, in the organizing and protesting and plotting and collaborating, whether or not the political goal is obtained. In the midst of the Montgomery bus boycott, when success was far from certain, Martin Luther King, Jr., told assembled protesters, "I want you to know that this struggle has not been in vain. . . . If it has done any one thing in this community it has given us a new sense of dignity." Dignity was in the struggle.[10]

In Douglass's case, struggle means a physical, bodily struggle against his master. With his whole being involved in struggle, risking death, he is transformed. But he does not struggle alone. His fellow slaves risk punishment, perhaps their lives, to side with him. And he does not just struggle against Covey: Covey's cousin also grapples with him. Even when it seems as if struggle is a quintessentially individual act, it draws on a community and it aims not at defeating one individual but at dismantling the hold of a system. Further, struggle, and the dignity performed in struggle, is contagious. Normally the other slaves would have followed Covey's orders without question. But seeing Douglass's defiance, the illusion of their master's omnipotence was unmasked. When Covey sought to exercise his will over them, they also struggled. Their struggle took a different form from Douglass's. It was not bodily struggle, though it made their bodies vulnerable to harm. One of those slaves, Bill, at first pretends not to understand Covey. Then he redirects Covey's entreaties. Bill says yes, indeed, he does want to work. When Covey tells him that, in that moment, his job is to bind Douglass, Bill turns legalistic. He has been rented to Covey by his own master, and the terms of that agreement permit farm work, not punishing slaves. Here we have on display a variety of forms of struggle: not only with bodies but with other performances, with pretended ignorance and confusion, then with reasoning. Struggle can also be performed with the imagination, as new worlds free of domination are created in the mind; with aesthetic performance, as the master's ordering of the senses and emotions is brought into question; or through intellectual work, as the beliefs the master depends on are exposed as lies.[11]

Often when we think of struggle, we think of the difficult quest to obtain a particular object: the struggle to win or complete a race, to lose weight, to finish college while working a full-time job. When struggle aims at a particular object, let us call that *ontic* struggle. For the slave, the world is determined by the master. Each object in the slave's world is owned by the master. Each object in our world, where our perception and action are shaped by interlocking systems of domination, is constituted by those regimes of domination. The struggle to obtain any object may or may not be reasonable, and reflecting on such reasonableness may be important work, but the criteria of reasonableness are determined by systems of domination. Ontic struggle will not get us free; only *ontological* struggle, struggle aimed at domination, struggle against the master, promises us that. Even struggle against oppression, exploitation, and harm is not necessarily a site of dignity. But every struggle against domination involves dignity. *Domination* means the capacity of one to arbitrarily exercise her will on another. Paradigmatically, domination names the relationship of a master to a slave. The master is not, at every moment, commanding a slave to do this or that, whip in hand, yet he is at every moment the master. Domination is defined by a capacity to act rather than by specific acts. One who is enslaved may never be flogged, but the whip still stands as a symbol of that relationship of domination.[12]

Some interpreters of Douglass's fight with Covey take his desired object to be recognition. He wants to be seen as a human being by Covey and the world, as equal in standing to all other humans. On this view, dignity is indeed achieved through struggle, but the struggle is to achieve proper recognition—impossible in a world where some are masters and others are slaves. However, this confuses the slave's object in struggle. Douglass wants to be free from Covey's domination; whether Covey recognizes or does not recognize him is secondary. Douglass certainly does not want to be recognized as a fellow master, as a man capable of owning slaves. To desire recognition in the world is to accept that the world has the final say in matters of recognition when the world is infected by domination. To succeed in such a struggle is to succeed in achieving the position of master, which is no success at all. When struggle is understood to aim at recognition, it is given an ontic rather than an ontological meaning.

Crucially, the object of ontological struggle is, by definition, impossible to achieve. Covey can never set Douglass free. In the closed world of slave and master, struggle against the master will never obtain its end. Yet despite its manifest impossibility, that end continues to animate struggle. Temporally, the world remains closed, a future of freedom is impossible, but in another sense the world opens. In the process of struggle, freedom can be dreamed, and such dreams call into question the absolute control of the master—motivating more struggle. In our much more complex world, ontological struggle also aims at an impossible object, a world free of systems of domination. If the object of struggle were obtainable, if there were a path we could plot from here to there, it would not be the object that we truly desire. It would be just another worldly object, brought into being by systems of domination. It would be ontic, not ontological.

Domination extends from a specific interpersonal relationship—master and slave—to a system, obfuscating its origins and mechanism. In the starkest forms of slavery, persuading a person that another person can be treated as a slave requires an enormous apparatus of ideas, habits, feelings, institutions, and laws that conspire to make one class of people appear less than human. The Atlantic slave trade added a physical difference to the conspiracy, resulting in the package known as racialization. Even when one element is suspended, such as the legal regime of slavery, the apparatus persists, and it is the whole apparatus that creates the relationship of domination. The violence that symbolizes that relationship persists, but in new forms. Lynching replaces flogging, prison replaces lynching, the policeman's gun replaces the nightstick, which replaces the convict lease system. The symbols are impermanent, but the psychic and social work they perform is consistent, reinforcing systems of racial domination that constitute the afterlives of slavery that persist into the present. When domination is understood as an expansive apparatus that includes ideas, habits, feelings, institutions, and laws, struggle against it can take place in any of these dimensions. Domination persists when enough of the elements of the apparatus work together, sustaining ideas or feelings or laws that authorize, for example, anti-Black racism, against which Black people struggle through music or protest or tactical silence. This is the essence of dignity.

The proper object of struggle, in the ontological sense, is domination, recognizable because it necessarily involves the arbitrary exercise of one's will over another. In the primal scene of domination, the master's will is the overriding reality. In the world at large, often there is no one person standing as master, so there may seem to be no will involved. Focusing on the arbitrary exercise of individual will can even mislead: it can draw our attention to the bad apple, the police officer who is disproportionately harassing Black motorists or the boss who dismisses applicants with Black-sounding names, rather than the system of domination in which those individuals play a part. In most cases, no one individual is clearly in a position of domination—for example, with respect to the toxic air that clouds Black neighborhoods, the wealth gap between Black and white households, or the discomfort at an all-white party when a Black friend-of-a-friend shows up. Those who see these situations as instances of anti-Blackness tend to speak of the culpability of a system of racism, oppression, or domination. Their language is necessarily vague, requiring us to imagine the system, in a sense, imposing its will on individuals.

Instead of conjuring an abstract system and then anthropomorphizing it, a better approach is to toggle between the primal scene of domination, such as the one described by Douglass, and the complexities of the real world. If we can tell the right kind of story, linking that primal scene with a set of practices in the real world, we will have identified the one whose will looms over the life of another. In that primal scene, it is obviously Covey's will that can be arbitrarily imposed on Douglass. (In fact, moving from an abstract primal scene to Douglass's world already introduces complexities: Covey is also an instrument in a system, enlisted by Douglass's owner.) It then becomes an empirical task to fill in the details of purported domination in any given context, demonstrate how they are linked into a system, and show how that system is structurally homologous to the primal scene of domination. In this way, domination points to an ontological condition, rooted in its primal scene, whereas concepts like oppression, suffering, exploitation, injustice, and marginalization point to ontic conditions, specific harms in the world. For clarity in analysis and struggle, concepts like oppression must be translated into domination; in the process, some instances of oppression will not qualify and other instances of domination will come to light.[13]

Domination infects the world, but it conceals itself, making it appear that there is no domination at all and that all that matters is the ontic, not the ontological register. One means of concealment is naturalization. The way things are is the way they have always been: it is the way of the world, the way things must be. Whites are masters and Blacks are slaves. Whites are responsible and Blacks are prone to criminality. Whites are better at science and Blacks are better at dancing. Another means of concealment: to make it seem as though social practice and norms are all there is, as though all that matters is what is done and what ought to be done. There may be serious problems, knots in the makeup of our world, but they can be fixed through immanent critique. We just must name our deeply held values, such as treating everyone equally, and use these to inform the changes in our norms needed to solve problems like racism. But anti-Blackness is baked into the constitution of our world. It is not a discrete problem that can be solved.[14]

Struggle against domination means struggle against amorphous but deeply entrenched systems that include racial domination. The relationship between white master and Black slave in the Atlantic world represents domination at its purest, and this is why struggle against racial domination is the paradigm of struggle—and Black dignity is the paradigm of dignity (and Black philosophy is the starting point of all philosophy). This is why *Black* deserves an uppercase "B": it marks the ontological sense of domination made visible by Black slavery. There are, of course, other forms of domination, such as colonial domination (marked by military and police violence), patriarchy (marked by rape), and capitalism (marked by the violence accompanying poverty). There are metropolitan elites, men, and bosses who function as slave-masters, however much they might wish to distance themselves from that role. Forms of domination are certainly interconnected, and there is dignity in struggle against each, but nowhere else is the mechanism of domination as precise as in anti-Black racism. Never can we be as confident about correctly identifying dignity as when we identify Black dignity.

But just because we privilege one primal scene of domination, Black slave and white master, that does not make anti-Blackness separable from other systems of domination. We suffer from many diseases at once, and we will never be disease-free. Each ailment qualifies as a system of domination if a story can be told linking it to its primal scene: rape as the primal scene of patriarchy, indigenous dispossession as the primal scene of settler colonialism, the theft of labor-power as the primal scene of capitalism, and so on. Any object in the world is simultaneously constituted by multiple interlocking systems of domination. Most of the time, when we navigate the world in ordinary life, we bracket this ontological register and so may forget that it exists. When we attend to the struggle against domination, clarifying our target and tactics, we must pay attention to the ontological register, sometimes moving our analysis quickly among multiple primal scenes of domination.

The world is full of myriad interlocking systems of domination, some novel, some vestigial. Because domination is part of the constitution of the world, it never goes away, though any particular system of domination can diminish to the point that it no longer makes sense to speak about the primal scene of that system because it is no longer linked to the world by any compelling story (for example, British domination over the American colonies). There is no comprehensive list of the systems of domination affecting the world. One component of struggle is storytelling about domination, and what counts or does not count as a discrete system of domination depends on which stories can be compellingly told linking the system to the primal scene. It may emerge that what seemed like two systems of domination are actually one, or vice versa, or that an entirely new system of domination has come into being. The closer a system of domination is, in its ontic manifestations, to its primal scene, the more clarity and confidence we have in naming it. We have the most clarity about anti-Blackness.

So here we have Black dignity: struggle against domination. This account of dignity contrasts sharply with other accounts in circulation.

In one story of dignity's history, once upon a time, before modernity, dignity referred to the honors and privileges of high rank. Dignity was had by kings and nobles, church leaders and government officials. It was an attribute of dignitaries. Dukes or bishops or judges of equal rank had equal dignity. Then, in the late eighteenth century, according to political theorist Jeremy Waldron, there was a "transvaluation of values." Now ordinary people were granted dignity, while the dignity of nobles was found to be "superficial or bogus." In the modern world, all human beings are thought to share the same rank, and their common humanity gives all equal dignity. This democratized sense of dignity was embraced after the Second World War in the United Nations Charter, the Universal Declaration of Human Rights, and the constitutions of 142 countries.[15]

The sense of dignity found in today's racial justice movement resembles neither the premodern nor the modern concepts. It does not pick out classes of elites and name their status. Quite the opposite: from the perspective of Black dignity, dignitaries have the hollow appearance of dignity. In theory, a dignitary participates in some system of domination, is some form of master—and so is void of dignity. (The world is more complicated than any theory, of course.) Nor does the modern concept of dignity fit, for from the perspective of Black movements not every human being shares in dignity equally. Some people have more and some less. Some people are aligned with masters (even some of the enslaved are aligned with masters), and thus have no dignity at all. Only those aligned with the enslaved struggling against domination have dignity. In a sense, Black dignity inverts the aristocratic hierarchy, elevating the lowliest and demoting the highest. Harriet Tubman, Angela Davis, and Assata Shakur have dignity; Thomas Jefferson, John D. Rockefeller, and the queen of England have none.

But in two senses, Black dignity is fundamentally committed to equality, and to the equal distribution of dignity. Struggle against domination is motivated by a vision of a world without domination. Though that world is presently inaccessible, we have a foretaste of it in the expansive practices of struggle—political organizing, dancing, dreaming. In that envisioned world, where every system of domination is dismantled, there will be equality. The physical signs of domination are bowing one's head, averting one's eyes; once domination is no more, we will all look each other in the eyes and hold our heads high. But there is no path from our world to that world, for our world is so full of interlocking systems of domination that if we were to imagine such a path, as many do, it would already be infected by the ideas, feelings, habits, and values of some present system of domination. The only way to access it, and then only imperfectly, is in a different register, through poetry or art or song.[16]

The other sense in which Black dignity is fundamentally committed to equality is in the view that systems of domination are so expansive, so numerous, so interconnected, that we are each, all of the time, both master and slave. Even the most marginalized subject—in caricature, the queer, poor, Black, disabled, immigrant woman—has been formed in a world of homophobia, capitalism, white supremacy, ableism, and xenophobia that have shaped her ideas, feelings, habits, and values. Even as she struggles to organize against the laws, norms, and institutions that dominate her, she will never fully purge herself of internalized oppression, which not only affects how she sees herself but also helps perpetuate the systems of domination that place others in the role of slave. Conversely, even the most privileged person is, in some aspect of his life, struggling against domination in some form. This is the human condition: we are at once master and slave, enjoying some benefits of privilege and struggling against some who have privilege. Our struggles are not only external, against laws and institutions, but internal, against our own malformed habits, feelings, and values. In this sense, we all participate in dignity because we all struggle against domination. Orders of magnitude separate the types and degree of struggles required of different people, but the struggle against domination is part of the human condition. We all have a taste of dignity, and it primes us for more—to participate in struggles with others, to challenge even the most entrenched systems of domination. But to discern dignity and to clarify how it is manifest requires routing our analysis through the ultimate paradigm of dignity, Blackness.

Multiculturalism obscures the meaning of Black dignity, but the era of multiculturalism is over. The Black Lives Matter movement signals a decisive shift to a new way of understanding Blackness.

Multiculturalism arose out of a desire to institutionalize—and, consciously or not, contain and control—struggles for racial justice. With multiculturalism triumphant, every high school student learns of the heroism of civil rights protesters, every college freshman reads Toni Morrison's *Beloved*, and every corporate executive knows that embracing diversity must be one of the organization's core values. From kindergarten to nursing homes, multicultural nights feature colorful clothes, tasty foods, and distinctive crafts. A Black man was elected president of the United States.[17]

By "multiculturalism" I don't mean the fact of cultural diversity or legal claims about group rights, but a set of ideas and practices about how different people ought to live together. Multiculturalism is about *managing* diversity by reducing political claims about domination to claims about the need to recognize and celebrate diverse cultures, offering up, in the words of activist Lynice Pinkard, only "bite-sized elements of culture." The Black Panthers' ten-point program for social transformation is largely forgotten; their black leather jackets and berets are remembered and blend seamlessly with Black nationalists' invention of Kwanzaa, the songs of Aretha Franklin, and the prose of James Baldwin—which sit together on a shelf (or calendar or booth) next to Latino cultural artifacts, Asian American cultural artifacts, and Native American cultural artifacts. This takes place in a framework compatible with political liberalism, where each individual has the freedom to choose which holidays to celebrate, which dances to learn, which foods to cook, which clubs to join, which person to marry, and which children to adopt. Multiculturalism demands that we suspend judgment about the goodness, truth, and beauty contained in any culture. And it treats our own culture as one option among many, rather than as the value-laden community in which we have been formed. But note: because white American culture is itself committed to multiculturalism, to imaging itself value-free, there is an alignment between the values of that particular culture and the broader multiculturalist framework. Black Americans, meanwhile, feel the full force of the tension between the unequivocally value-laden nature of Black culture and the value-neutral framework of multiculturalism.[18]

Today, multiculturalism is the provincial discourse of diversity professionals at corporations and universities, and of schoolteachers. It is dismissed on the political right and center as "identity politics" and superseded on the left by new political discourses that affirm Blackness, indigenous sovereignty, and socialism.

Multiculturalism flourished in the United States when public discourse did not distinguish between "left" and "liberal," and it contributed to that confusion. (That both were identified with the Democratic Party, and that actual socialist organizations in the United States were nearly invisible to mainstream media, furthered this confusion.) At long last, with the rising visibility of movements that clearly reject and are rejected by liberalism, mainstream America is recognizing that *left* and *liberal* name different sets of political commitments. For Americans whose youth was marked by the financial crisis and Occupy Wall Street, liberalism holds little appeal. Yet even as more Americans have an intuitive affinity with the left and as energetic political movements on the left proliferate, leftist political philosophy remains inchoate. In *Jacobin* and *n + 1*, on public radio and at nonprofits' leadership retreats, there is talk of intersectionality, of the Black radical tradition, of New Age spiritual values, of decolonizing culture, of old-school Marxism and of Marxism informed by the Global South. There is also talk of left populism, which only confuses the conversation.

In fact, those on the left are animated by commitments to dramatic social transformation in the direction of justice. Put another way, they are committed to collectively struggling against domination. Black dignity names that struggle. Having emerged in Black social movements, the political philosophy of Black dignity could give the left coherence and vision.

The era of multiculturalism is over. The protests spawned by the murder of Trayvon Martin in 2012 broke multiculturalism's stranglehold on public discourse about diversity. Young Black people responded in a language that unequivocally affirmed Blackness and acknowledged the specificity and permanence of anti-Black racism. Demands for justice could no longer be satisfied by talk of law enforcement professionals doing their jobs more effectively, of prosecutors and judges acting better, or of laws being revised. Even the desiccated meaning justice had acquired, as the proper operation of the law, was given the lie as protesters called for imagining a world purged of racial domination. Black demands for justice expanded to include calls to imagine the impossible, such as prison abolition and reparations for slavery. In 2020, the protests against police violence sparked by George Floyd's murder led to calls to abolish police departments. And this style of politics, organizing around demands for the seemingly impossible, for justice beyond what is legible from a policy-oriented perspective, has spread beyond Black politics. It shows up, for example, in resurgent indigenous rights activism, in demands for universal access to health care and free college tuition, and in demands to reckon with colonial legacies worldwide.

Barack Obama's presidency pushed multiculturalism to its limits and exposed how vacuous it is. If King's civil rights discourse was eclipsed during a march in which Stokely Carmichael shouted, "Black power!," Obama's discourse of multiculturalism was eclipsed on Facebook. On July 13, 2013, California-based labor organizer Alicia Garza learned that the killer of seventeen-year-old Trayvon Martin had been acquitted by a Florida jury. "I was sad, I was angry," she reports. She posted her reflections on Facebook, and her friend Patrisse Cullors, a prison reform organizer, responded, "#blacklivesmatter." The phrase went viral, not only on social media but in the wider culture through the concerted efforts of Garza, Cullors, and Opal Tometi, leader of the Black Alliance for Just Immigration. They set up Tumblr and Twitter accounts to disseminate the hashtag, put the phrase on posters, and created a network of local groups across the United States and beyond.[19]

The Black Lives Matter movement transformed the vocabulary of racial justice. No longer are African Americans one of many cultural groups within the rainbow of American diversity. Now, Blackness is unequivocally affirmed on its own. So is the qualitative difference between anti-Black racism, fueled by slavery's afterlives, and all other forms of ethnic or racial discrimination. The Movement for Black Lives platform emerged through extensive consultation with grassroots organizers to build consensus around a shared vision. The opening words of the platform are "Black humanity and dignity requires Black political will and power." This was not a return to the language of Black power but an affirmation of Blackness attentive to the margins, centering the voices and experiences of Blacks who are women, queer, trans, undocumented, disabled, incarcerated, and poor. The platform demands "Black self-determination and community control," affirms "holistic healing," condemns "patriarchy," demands the abolition of prisons, and calls for an end to investment in fossil fuels—all under the banner of affirming Blackness. Black Lives Matter political organizing brought a far-reaching cultural shift. Black Americans now regularly affirm Black love, Black rage, Black girl magic, Black excellence, and Black bodies. Beyoncé rhymes about how she likes "Afros" and her "negro nose" in a song about organizing Black women: "Now let's get in formation." The rapper D Smoke enumerates "Black Habits": Black hug, Black love, Black tie, Black ride, Black pride, and Black lives, reaching a climax with "everything Black." This has become the language of Black America.[20]

But do hashtags and song lyrics signal anything more than a cultural shift? I claim in this book that the new vocabulary of Black Lives Matter represents a new moral and political stance. The moral, political, and cultural here are deeply entangled. What may seem like rhetoric or performance—or a mere tweet—actually participates in a distinctive and coherent position. The cornerstone of that position is affirmation of Black dignity, and reflection on Black dignity demonstrates the coherence of the new Black vocabulary. The new "Black habits" are not merely new ways of talking or acting. They articulate a philosophy, a set of ideas about how the world is. This philosophy flows from the claim to Black dignity.

In a narrow sense, philosophy is the work of professional philosophers: scholars who make their livings teaching and writing about the big questions of truth, goodness, and beauty—or, more often, developing technical idioms for approaching those questions. In a more expansive sense, "philosophy" refers to a community's core commitments, those ideas about what exists and what matters that are broadly held but not often made explicit, except by outsiders intrigued by "Navajo philosophy," "African philosophy," or "Chinese philosophy." Of course, the

American academics who claim philosophy as a profession, for all their claims of objectivity, offer a specialized vocabulary for describing deeply held American commitments of the age—as do the French, the Germans, and all others. The American philosopher cares about clear writing, problem-solving, and useful distinction-making; the French philosopher cares about the passions, grandiloquence, and radical posturing; the German about system, fidelity to past masters, and rectitude. Obviously these are caricatures, but they are based in reality. Philosophers breathe the same air as everyone else, and the philosophy of a people finds expression not only in their and other scholars' works but in the works of poets, singers, and novelists—in Melville, Thoreau, and David Foster Wallace; in Voltaire and Camus and Michel Houellebecq; in Goethe and Wagner and Thomas Mann. In cultural production, philosophy is expressed as it is contested, and we are invited into the great contest of ideas about truth, goodness, and beauty that defines a community.

Black dignity is the philosophy of Black Americans, but it is also more. To see it as something provincial and race-based is to fall back into the language of multiculturalism. From a multiculturalist perspective, each community has its philosophy, and we ought to revel in the variety—and especially in expanding the pantheon. But Black dignity stands in opposition to multiculturalism. I stand with Black dignity. You must choose. The set of habits and ideas whose coherence is named by Black dignity is incommensurable with other philosophies, as well as with the ostensibly value-neutral perspective of multiculturalism that flattens all traditions to fit into their separate colorful booths at the diversity fair. One view is right; others might seem right but are wrong. One view names goodness; others seem to name goodness but actually commend the bad and condemn the good. One view names beauty; others name the simulacrum of beauty. The stakes are high: when the revolution comes, or the rapture, I sure as hell don't want to be standing next to you unless you believe in Black dignity.

While Black dignity is made more visible by the eclipse of multi-culturalism, dignity has long been at the heart of Black political organizing and Black life. The process of organizing a social movement brings clarity to the participants' intuitions. As they collectively reflect on their experiences of struggle, their views sharpen, not only on first-order questions in the struggle itself but on second-order questions about truth, goodness, and beauty—about philosophy. This is what the Black Lives Matter movement offers us: distilled wisdom from Black struggles of the past years, decades, and centuries, sharpened by the most immediate struggle. We see and speak and feel today more, and more precisely, than we once could because our discontent with the ideology of multiculturalism brings these histories of struggle into sharp relief. Taking stock of these insights, often implicit in movement discourse, lays the groundwork for further refinement in the years of struggle ahead.

Thanks in part to social media, in part to the collapsing academic job market, our current political moment is unique in the speed with which academic theories enter into social movement spaces and vocabularies. This is particularly true in Black Lives Matter–adjacent political spaces. Two streams of theory circulate in these spaces, each emphasizing that Blackness is not one among many racial or ethnic differences but qualitatively different and unique. Both streams, in other words, are diametrically opposed to multiculturalism. One stream focuses on the exclusion of Blackness from the world, the other on the liberating potential of embracing Blackness.[21]

Afropessimism is a term used loosely—even more loosely when it travels from scholarly to activist spaces—to refer to the claim that Blackness (not only Black people but everything associated with Black people, even the color black) is systematically and constitutively excluded from the world. This position welds a historical claim to a metaphysical claim. Historically, the African slave trade shaped the ideas and desires of the entire Western world in such a way that everything associated with Blackness was denigrated and yet necessary for that world to function. For the European and North American cultures of modernity to develop, and for their economies to develop, they needed an "other," not a distant other but one that was nearby and yet impossible to assimilate. Black people were at once present and obviously human, but not counted as human; maintaining this paradox required a great deal of cultural and psychic work. Blackness became feared and desired, loathsome and titillating, invisible and hypervisible. The cultural and psychic mechanisms of anti-Blackness persisted through the afterlives of slavery, the eras of Jim Crow and mass incarceration. They are required for the European- and North American–dominated world order to maintain itself. This means Blackness is different from any other racial or ethnic identity, for those identities can grow or fade as circumstances change. They function now as junior partners to whiteness. Latinos and Asian Americans can achieve the status of honorary whites, and eventually gain entry into an expanded category of whiteness, as Jewish Americans and Italian Americans did. The possibility of assimilation is forever closed to Blacks. This conclusion is borne out not just by reflection on culture and psyches but by statistics: in the United States, the average net worth of a white family is ten times that of a Black family, and the likelihood of incarceration is an order of magnitude higher for Black people. Poverty rates, infant mortality rates, pollution exposure levels, employment access, and much else show that the enormous disadvantages faced by Blacks persist well after the end of the legal regimes of slavery and segregation. Even school integration, iconic of the promise of legally mandated equality, is by some measures worse today than it was in 1954, when the Supreme Court struck down school segregation laws.[22]

For Afropessimists, the practice of anti-Blackness authorizes and is authorized by derogatory ideas about Blacks. Enlightenment philosophers and America's founding fathers were notorious for their anti-Black racism even as they proclaimed universal freedom and equality. From Kant to Hegel to Thomas Jefferson, ostensibly race-neutral claims about human nature, the nature of reality, and the meaning of goodness sat alongside claims about the subhuman nature of Blacks. And these thinkers stand in for a broader swath of ideas that characterize modernity throughout the world, with metaphysics matching microaggressions and overt anti-Black violence. Afropessimist views began to coalesce in California in the wake of the 1992 Rodney King uprising, when activists and academics were calling for progressives to work together in multiracial coalitions. Two Black graduate students at Berkeley, Frank Wilderson and Jared Sexton, felt that the focus on multiracial coalition-building ignored the specificity of the anti-Black racism they felt on their minds and bodies. They synthesized several strands of theory into a project that refused multiculturalism, and refused hope. The depths of anti-Blackness were too great to be remedied by policy reform.

If Afropessimism tells a sad story, advocates of fugitivity largely accept the same theoretical framework but tell a happy story. Led by the prolific poet and theorist Fred Moten, they use the term *fugitivity* to name the possibilities for flourishing in a world of anti-Blackness. Whereas Afropessimists identify with the slave and the neoslave, advocates of fugitivity identify with the maroon, once a slave but now on the run, creating new forms of community in hidden mountain valleys or underground jazz clubs. If modernity refuses humanity to Blacks, then modernity's concept of humanity is stale and hollow. Black life is lived in the shadows, in the interstices, ducking and diving and jiving and improvising, creating cultural and aesthetic productions that can never be assimilated to the world of white supremacy, the world of modernity. These stories, jokes, songs, poems, and front porch conversations constitute Blackness and demonstrate its life-giving richness. If the world would treat Blackness as social death, the severing of all family and community relations in and after the Middle Passage, Blackness names the social life of social death, the joyous ingenuity of a death-bound people.[23]

Like Afropessimism and fugitivity, Black dignity accepts the qualitative difference between anti-Black racism and other forms of racial and ethnic discrimination. Unlike Afropessimism, Black dignity is not primarily invested in explaining anti-Blackness by reference to history or metaphysics, although it may use them to illuminate a system of domination operating in the present. Blackness is privileged not because of gruesome facts or the configuration of ideas but because it points to the purest form of domination. Similarly, from the perspective of Black dignity, Black sociality does not name the ideal of human flourishing. Dignity is to be found in life lived under conditions of domination, but not all such life has dignity. We are required to assess which elements of Black aesthetics and sociality are directed against domination. Not all jazz improv sessions are created equal, nor are all barbershop conversations. Moreover, where advocates of Afropessimism and fugitivity take Blackness as a solid foundation, even as the content of that Blackness is elusive or dynamic or ineffable, Black dignity finds its foundation in the multiplicity of interlocking forms of domination. We must choose the political and theoretical tools that are appropriate to struggle against whatever forms of domination are salient in a specific time and place, even as analysis of domination achieves its greatest clarity when routed through domination's chief paradigm, Blackness.

While academic theories affirming the specificity of anti-Blackness are increasingly prevalent in activist spaces, most scholarly work on race remains stuck in a cultural studies model—and so is largely ignored by those engaged in political struggle. The monumental and antiquarian forms of writing history that Friedrich Nietzsche decried more than a century ago, which draw pleasure from celebrating or enumerating events of the past so as to affirm the status quo in the present, have returned today with the reduction of radicalism to a brand or a slogan. Simply naming voices and practices that have been excluded from the canon is seen as political work. It certainly is work that offers pleasure, but too often it is the same pleasure Nietzsche saw as affirming the status quo. Today's status quo is multiculturalism. More "critical" cultural studies scholars not only celebrate or enumerate diverse cultures but do so in a framework that is meant to unmask the machinations of the powerful and to model ways of living against the grain. The scholar's task is to reveal ideologies of homophobia, transphobia, racism, misogyny, ableism, and nationalism in cultural artifacts, sometimes all lumped together as "normativity," and this act of unmasking generates its own pleasure. In a complementary move, scholarly attention has turned to celebrating "relationality" displayed in cultural artifacts—that is, how humans relate to each other and to the world intimately, fluidly, imaginatively, unconstrained by the concepts and grids that "normativity" (or modernity, or whiteness, or settler colonialism) imposes on the world. With relationality, cultural studies scholars derive pleasure from inverted monumentalism, finding in the most marginal voices, such as queer indigenous writers, resources for supposedly overturning the status quo.[24]

These views leave little space for genuine judgment. Normativity is reduced to a binary: good or bad, fluid or rigid, porous or closed, invested in the status quo or contesting it, in harmony with the wisdom of nature and the ancestors or aligned with violent Western capitalist hetero-patriarchy. The binary choice is presupposed, and the scholar's task is simply to place a given cultural artifact on the correct side of the divide. The powerful and correct insight fueling such projects is that

domination conceals itself, and attacking systems of domination requires naming those systems' cultural manifestations and subterfuges.
But the projects go wrong when they confuse discrete systems of domination, each rooted in a primal scene of master and slave, with abstract
ideologies. This confusion leads the critic to condemn all normativity,
all judgments about what ought or ought not to be done. Such a stance
complements multiculturalism's refusal to speak in terms of *ought* and
ought not, its affirmation of the right of each person and each community to speak and act in their distinctive manner. The cultural studies
scholar aligns herself with the anti-normativity of multiculturalism
against the supposed crypto-normativity of modernity, but in doing so
deprives herself of the ability to struggle against specific forms of domination. For the cultural studies scholar, power is everywhere and struggle is everywhere; to target a particular form of domination would be to
obscure those fundamental facts.[25]

In contrast, Black studies entered universities through collective
struggle aligned with the Black power movement. Black students and
faculty demanded scholarship that participates in struggle against racial domination, and they wanted Black studies to be treated as a
privileged site of struggle against domination as such. The purpose of
Black studies was not simply to reflect on the racism of the existing
canon, or to expand the canon to include more Black voices. It was
envisioned as a new form of scholarly engagement that involved, first
and foremost, integration in and accountability to broader Black
communities organizing against racial domination. Student activists
demanded that Black studies programs report to community advisory
boards that would keep those programs properly oriented. And Black
studies programs would incubate scholarship that expanded the
meaning of rigor. Given that racial domination extends to the realm
of scholarly knowledge and modes of inquiry, struggle against racial
domination in the context of a university meant attending to feelings

and not just reasons, to ways of imagining and not just ways of debating. Black studies programs aimed to disrupt the hegemony of hollow technical knowledge in the North American academy by pursuing the genuine truth, goodness, and beauty that the world repeatedly denied.[26]

That is, they used to. One story about the withering aspirations of Black studies as an academic field over the past half century has to do with the institutionalization and corporatization of the university. The ambition to do scholarship differently faded away as Black studies departments came under increasing pressure to look like every other university program and department, and as universities increasingly viewed students as customers and education as a consumer product. Perversely, the success of the midcentury fight against legal segregation also made possible the ethos of multiculturalism that castrated Black studies. With historically white institutions now open to Black students and new career trajectories open to the Black middle class, there was increasing physical and social separation between Blacks having different amounts of economic and social capital. Whereas Black intellectuals, artists, and blue-collar workers once lived in close proximity, now a small group of "promising" Blacks go to predominantly white colleges, spend their professional careers in predominantly white businesses and organizations, and live in predominantly white neighborhoods. While the assimilation of any minority ethnic group produces similar dynamics, the ongoing pressure of racial domination felt by Black Americans intensified the dissonance between formation in and allegiance to Black family and community, on one hand, and school and work in white institutions, on the other. This tension, certainly difficult for all who experience it, created grave pathologies for those whose profession is to speak about Blackness. One minute, the professor is on the golf course with his white colleagues, the next moment he is fielding a call from his incarcerated cousin, and the next moment he is explaining the nuances of Black poetry to predominantly white students. This is an unstable position, and one that heightens eccentricities or worse. To try to meld such individuals into a scholarly community organized around a shared commitment to intellectual struggle against racial domination is nearly impossible. (It is telling that the most powerful theoretical innovations in Black studies in recent years, the Afropessimist and fugitivity frameworks, originated and primarily circulate outside Black studies departments.) Given these pressures, Black scholarship in the era of multiculturalism drifted further and further from grassroots political organizing.[27]

Academic philosophy departments, reached late by multiculturalism, have now realized that they should have something to say about Black people. At elite levels, this has mostly taken the form of attempts to clarify the concept of race. Does it properly refer to biology? Experiences of oppression? Shared culture? Does it differ from ethnicity? Black dignity turns this approach inside out. All philosophy must be routed through the Middle Passage. Philosophy begins in straining against shackles. Plato's allegory of the cave invites us to think about the truth (and goodness and beauty) that is overlooked when all are imprisoned, and the hollow illusions in that prison that substitute for truth. If we live in a world full of interlocking systems of domination that are each maintained by making the false seem true, we are all living in Plato's cave. In Plato's allegory, one freed prisoner drags himself to the light, first feeling pain and rage, then quickly learning to love seeing things themselves, in truth. The claim implicit in the racial justice movement is that collective struggle against the shackles of prison, slavery, or any form of domination brings clarity and wisdom. Through struggle we come to see truly. We come to recognize the ruses of domination, how it makes the bad appear good and the ugly appear beautiful. Through struggle, we come to experience a happiness that makes all earlier forms of happiness seem pitiful. Through struggle and *in* struggle, for the pervasiveness of domination means that struggle is never-ending. The shackles in the cave are but an allegory.[28]

Seen in this light, philosophy is not the domain of the individual but of the collective, of the social movement struggling against domination. Philosophy must be accountable to social movements, but its accountability is complex. Social movement organizers are necessarily focused on the tasks of gathering, educating, strategizing, targeting, assessing, and collaborating. They are at home in meetings and in protests, with flyers and sticky notes, press releases and chants. Philosophers have time to listen. They can note patterns and clarify concepts. They can reflect on movements against domination across history and around the world, and explicate the grammar of struggle. And they can attend to specific movements and movement vocabularies, drawing attention to ways those movements might speak in a language that follows this grammar of struggle. The preeminent mode of domination is anti-Blackness, slavery's afterlives, and the preeminent struggle is the Black struggle. Black philosophy must be the starting point of all philosophy.

The success of a philosophical project should not be judged by its internal consistency or how tight a system it forms, by its fit with commonly held intuitions or by its match with a certain community's convictions. C. L. R. James and his colleagues once wrote, "From Plato to Hegel, European philosophers were always struggling to make a total harmonious unity of societies riddled by class struggles. They were attempting the impossible, organizing in the mind what could only be organized in society." Unlike European philosophical traditions, Black dignity succeeds if its claims clearly and consistently flow out of the primal struggle against domination, and if they motivate collective organizing. Reasoning and rhetoric, histories and intuitions are all put to the service of explicating that primal scene of domination. In a world full of those who would impose their will on us, of masters and prison guards and bosses who conceal their domination of us, in a world where we ourselves have been formed in systems of domination that teach us to conceal our humanity from ourselves, how are we to claim our humanity? How can we embrace what we are beyond who we are? Privilege conceals these questions, offering comfort and insulation from the violence of domination, at most embracing struggle as an individual quest for self-realization—and so blocking off the possibility of flourishing, and genuine happiness. Those who are most marginalized feel domination most violently. It is in the collective struggles of the most marginalized against domination that we also find the only possibility of flourishing, of happiness—of Black joy.[29]

You interrupt. *But what am I to do?* You sympathize with Black struggle, you appreciate the unimaginable depths of anti-Blackness, your liberal heart aches, and you want to do the right thing. *What are the policy solutions? The educational campaigns? The new nonprofits that need to be formed? The listening sessions that need to be organized?* You who are titillated by my talk of dancing Black bodies, enchanted by the romance of struggle, pleasured by the impossible odds and the unimaginably high stakes, or speaking from genuine moral concern—you demand to know my political platform. You would prefer a numbered, prioritized list. But really you would be equally pleased to be told that the demands cannot be enumerated, the problem so grave only silent witness will suffice.

Moralizing and policymaking offer pleasures to both speaker and listener. Things are not right in the world. Now you know why, and how to respond. Your soul settles. After the urban uprisings that followed the killing of George Floyd by Minneapolis police officers, white liberal "allies" showed up the next morning with brooms and trash bags. Singly and in groups, they walked through my neighborhood sweeping up the broken glass and ashes. They were in no position to judge the rightness of the rebellion, they told themselves, but they knew they were guilty and needed to do penance.

In this book's afterword, I discuss specific ethical practices and principles implied by the account of Black dignity I develop, but I avoid both broad moralizing and policy prescription. Clear-headed analysis is needed, together with practical wisdom. Once we see the world rightly, we respond rightly, unmediated by dogma. Seeing the world rightly, clouded as it is by systems of domination, is a necessary but nearly impossible task. It requires a rigorous approach: this is what Black dignity teaches. Ultimately, rigor can be achieved only through critical accountability to social movements organizing against domination.

When we think about a movement, we often think in political terms, about claims and strategies and power. More important, but often overlooked, is the movement's moral vocabulary, the ideas about what is good, true, and beautiful that animate it. This book is about the ideas animating today's racial justice movement. I name these ideas the philosophy of Black dignity. The book is not a philosophical or historical analysis of the concept of dignity in Black life and thought; its focus is the movement. Dignity is one among several key concepts animating the movement, and it stands in for the whole. But dignity is more than synecdoche: understanding dignity in movement contexts, dignity in motion, sheds light on all the concepts that are part of the new moral vocabulary emerging around Black Lives Matter, and helps us see the coherence of this vocabulary.

Each of the five chapters that follow is devoted to one key concept in the philosophy of Black dignity, encapsulated in a hashtag. These five concepts are representative but not exhaustive. Reflecting on them provides insight into the moral orientation of the movement as a whole. This reflection begins by tracking exemplary uses of the concept by activists; it also reconstructs the grammar behind those uses, aided by critical dialogue with intellectuals formed by and embedded in the movement. Through this process, I pivot from the way we use these concepts in ordinary language to their quite different significance in movement contexts—to their ontological significance. In ordinary language, *rage* and *love* name emotions directed at particular people or things, *family* names close relatives, *futures* names times to come, and *magic* names the pretense of the supernatural. Today's racial justice movement diagnoses anti-Blackness as contaminating all aspects of our world, and the movement's vocabulary attempts to turn away from anti-Blackness—away from the contaminated world. *Black dignity* names not a status but rather the struggle against racial domination and the embrace of a forever distant, opaque possibility of a world without domination. *Black rage* does not fume at any particular instance of harm but at a system of domination any particular instance represents. *Black love* names the feeling of comradeship in struggle, not romance. *Black family* refers not to genetic or legal ties but to those joined by Black love in struggle. *Black futures* are not at the far end of a timeline; they label how we imagine a world without domination, across an unbridgeable divide from now and yet animating our struggle. To conjure such futures, interrupting the present, is to deploy *Black magic*.

In this approach I take inspiration from the Jewish philosopher Emmanuel Levinas. After surviving the Holocaust, Levinas found his world shattered, including its most fundamental concepts. The ordinary meanings of words rang hollow; conceiving of philosophy as an effort to refine concepts like freedom, enjoyment, justice, and love was at best useless, at worst making philosophy complicit in genocide. Instead, Levinas took the encounter with another human, gazing into the other's face, as "first philosophy"—the necessary starting point for all philosophical reflection that could evade complicity and could even challenge the world's genocidal ways. The task of philosophy became routing the analysis of any concept through that primordial encounter with the other, untethering concepts from their meanings in ordinary talk. Similarly, in the face of anti-Black racism, I argue that the task of philosophy is routing the analysis of concepts through a primordial encounter: the encounter between master and slave. I differ from Levinas, however, by taking a social movement for racial justice, rather than the Western philosophical tradition, as the primary guide for my analysis. I find concepts bending away from the world, in the direction of Black dignity, in the words of activists and organic intellectuals (those formed by and responsive to social movements); I do not engage with the thought of Kant, Hegel, or Heidegger.[30]

While at some points in this book I spotlight movement discourse and at other points I systematize that discourse, neither of those tasks is my ultimate goal. I am interested in a prophetic embrace of the ideas animating the movement. Activists are shaped by those ideas, but their rhetoric, produced in the heat of struggle and responsive to particular contexts, offers a starting point rather than an ending point. A systematic account of the movement's ideas can be a useful tool in clarifying and communicating those ideas, but the realm of abstract definitions and arguments drifts away from a relationship of accountability to on-the-ground organizing. In each chapter, therefore, I move between these two registers, modeling a process of discernment that is sharpened by my arguments with organic intellectuals whose assessments of the Black political tradition sometimes miss the mark. To participate in a tradition means to argue with those close to it, not simply to compile their ideas. Whether it is Martin Luther King, Jr., or bell hooks, Frederick Douglass or Audre Lorde, each organic intellectual is at times closer to the core of a tradition, at times further from that core—over the course of a life, or even within the same text. My task is to hold up examples of organic intellectuals getting it right, hewing closely to the philosophy of Black dignity implicit in the movement, and equally, to call out moments when organic intellectuals go astray or when multiculturalism obscures their insights. In short, developing an account of Black dignity requires judgment. Judgment is a crucial form of struggle.

What, precisely, is the movement for racial justice? Black Lives Matter is a hashtag, a network of grassroots organizations, and a label now applied expansively to all mobilizations for racial justice. Doing justice to it requires recognizing organizing work and infrastructure that is often invisible in media representations of the movement. The book's final chapter considers the shape of revolutionary social movements today, in an age when abolitionism, socialism, and community organizing have gone mainstream. In each chapter, I examine the words of activists and organic intellectuals, but I also engage with the thought of the movement's ancestors. The struggle against racial domination did not begin this decade. Recounting its many stories is an important project, but it is not my project. I call up the ancestors who are invoked in movement spaces and texts, critically engaging with their thought, in order to hold myself accountable to the movement today. (I take accountability to be an imperative to critical engagement, not veto power.) These reflections, being guided by movement discourse rather than chronology or national boundaries, move thematically between today's activists and different historical figures, and between U.S.-based thinkers and those abroad. But I share the movement's implicit commitment, which forms the cornerstone of the philosophy of Black dignity: that the struggle against domination has an essential structure. This structure cannot be expressed in a list of premises and conclusions; it can only be discerned through critical engagement with the movement. That is the task of the pages that follow.

2

Black Rage

The era of multiculturalism ended in the United States on February 26, 2012. On that day, seventeen-year-old Trayvon Martin was shot to death by neighborhood watch coordinator George Zimmerman. The Black teenager was visiting relatives in a gated community in Sanford, Florida. He went out, wearing jeans and a hoodie, to get candy from a nearby store. On his way home he was spotted by Zimmerman, who called the police to report a suspicious person. Zimmerman followed Martin and killed him in what Zimmerman would later claim was self-defense.

Over the next month, protests against Martin's killing multiplied. Students walked out of schools in Florida, young and old people rallied throughout the country, often wearing hoodies as a symbol of solidarity. Barack Obama offered a personal reflection: "If I had a son, he would look like Trayvon." The story of a Black boy shot for walking through a gated community disgusted and enraged many, and many Black Americans found the racial harassment and violence Martin experienced all too familiar. In gatherings at schools and universities, parks and courthouses, the anger of individual protesters became collective rage. As protesters talked together, in person and online, they discerned the source of their outrage: much more than George Zimmerman, it was the anti-Blackness that infected America. Protesters were angry at a system of domination that had been in place since the days of slavery, taking new forms but continuing to affect Black Americans' lives every day, from looks and comments to limited job opportunities and the wealth gap to blood pressure levels and exposure to environmental toxins.

The rage felt in March 2012 returned a year later when Zimmerman's murder trial resulted in a not-guilty verdict. It returned again, more intensely, in 2014 when eighteen-year-old Michael Brown was shot by a police officer in Ferguson, Missouri. The choreography of protest, in the decades of multiculturalism's reign, had emphasized steadfast nonviolence in a caricature of the civil rights movement. A notable exception—the response to Rodney King's videotaped beating in 1991 at the hands of Los Angeles police—was in a wholly different category: riot or uprising rather than protest. But beginning in 2012, the mood of Black protest was no longer pacific. In part this change had to do with the large proportion of youths among the protesters, in part with broader shifts in the culture of protest. Occupy Wall Street had started in 2011, and anger at the status quo, previously confined to left-wing fringes, was drawing a broader public. While the 2012 protests had mixed older activist repertoires with a new urgency and anger, in Ferguson the dominant mood was rage. Yes, there were candles and prayers, but even more there was venting and shouting and cursing, night after night.

Rage is contagious, but it is not formless. It takes shape as it spreads, as the anger of individuals resonates with others who are angry, and as the wrongs anger tracks become clearer. Polemicists, speakers, and artists not only echo and amplify this anger but reflect and direct it, naming its objects. In 2012, Lauryn Hill began performing a new song, "Black Rage," and in August 2014, as protests in Ferguson were cresting, she released a recording of the song and posted the lyrics on her website. To a slow, sad remix of the Rodgers and Hammerstein song "My Favorite Things," Hill becomes Julie Andrews turned inside out. Capturing the mood of Black America, she sings with practiced dejection rather than delight. She is ornery rather than effervescent. Hill is angry, she knows others are angry, and she sings the causes of Black rage.[1]

The ultimate cause of Black rage is slavery. Hill's song opens,

> Black rage is founded on two-thirds a person
> Rapings and beatings and suffering that worsens
> Black human packages tied up in strings.

The legal and social practices accompanying slavery are the origins of Black rage, but the evils of slavery persist even after slavery is outlawed. Poverty and violence perdure. Beyond any of the specific evils faced by Black Americans, and at the root of them all, according to Hill, is something deeper: "Black rage is founded on wounds of the soul." When the soul is attacked, we respond with indignation; shared indignation turns into rage. Rage expressed, performed—sung—becomes dignity.

What are these "wounds of the soul"? Most basically, they come from being treated as less than human—to be precise, as two-thirds of a human (a riff on the Constitution counting enslaved Blacks as three-fifths of a person). Humans react to such treatment with indignity. But here is where things get worse, where the injury is compounded: for the enslaved, and those whose lives are shaded by slavery's afterlives, indignation is not permitted. As Hill sings, when Blacks voice our indignation, when we complain, we are called "mad" and our freedom is threatened. We are made not only to endure "lies and abuse" but to parrot them, to hate ourselves, to commit "spiritual treason." Hill has put her finger on one of the key mechanisms of domination. The threat of force only names the surface of domination; at its heart, it is about violence to souls, about making a human believe she is actually less than human, about making domination seem right and natural.

But domination never has the last word. The master never owns the souls of those he enslaves. Truth is still truth, and the master's lies, even when parroted and internalized by slaves, are still lies. Deep down we all know this. But rarely can we put it into the right words, for language itself has been turned into a tool of domination. Some can only grunt or gasp, laugh or scream: each is a marker of Black rage. Giving Black rage shape requires telling a story: naming connections between the seemingly disparate aspects of racial domination and giving an account of how they grow out of a primal scene of domination. Telling such a story in a world of anti-Blackness requires a different medium from straightforward exposition. It requires a medium like music, a song like Hill's. After "dog bites" and "beatings" and "feeling sad" comes the refrain, "I simply remember all these kinds of things and then I don't fear so bad."

But the effect of Hill's song is not only to lessen fear. It is to struggle, to perform struggle, to struggle in performance. Near the end of "Black Rage," she sings, "Try as you must but you can't have my soul / Black rage is made by ungodly control." Anti-Blackness attempts to seize the soul, but it fails, and this moment of failure brings deep equivocation. Anti-Blackness is an attempt at blasphemy, for the master to assume the role of God, to take "ungodly control" of another. But at the very same time, Black rage takes shape. It aims at that which attempts to dominate, and it marshals spiritual forces, "ungodly" forces, forces inexplicable in the terms of the anti-Black world, for struggle. As it takes shape, dignity is performed—and sung.

I feel angry when I am wronged or when I see something wrong. Anger is a moral thermometer. When I am feeling angry, I know something is morally amiss; when I am feeling very angry, I know something or someone is erring gravely. When someone breaks her promise to me, or deceives me, or harms me, I anger. When I read about innocents killed, or the elderly misled, or children left in harm's way, I anger.

If only it were so simple. Anger does track wrongs, but the cloud of human imperfections and worldly complications blocks the pathway from wrong inflicted to anger felt. I misperceive what is happening around me, who is causing it, and whether it really qualifies as a wrong. My anger ends up misdirected, or absent, or present at the wrong times or in the wrong quantities. Children's anger is wildly confused, with temper tantrums occasioned by the smallest perceived slights—but, through all the confusion, there is still, at root, a wrong, at least in the child's mind. The wildness of most adults' anger is tamed, but it is still, almost always, imperfectly calibrated and aimed. Imperfect, but meaningful: if anger is read correctly, we often find a genuine wrong that needs to be addressed.

When framed in this way, anger is felt alone by one individual. In the heart, anger can simmer, boil, boil over. The European canon begins with anger: it is the first word of the first great work of Western literature, the *Iliad*. The poem begins by calling on the goddess, the Muse, to sing of Achilles' anger, an anger that brought great difficulties and death to the Greeks. The *Iliad* is a song of vengeance and vendetta, each harm answered by a greater harm, all fueled by anger. Three hundred years later, Aeschylus would tell a quite different story about the same period of Greek history. In the *Eumenides*, Orestes is tormented by a personification of anger, the Furies. He committed a wrong, and the cycle of vengeance seems as if it will never end. But Athena ends the cycle by creating the first trial by jury in Athens, over which she presides. Establishing a legal system channels and controls anger, providing a means for discerning when and where genuine wrongs have been committed. Here we have the Western paradigm for dealing with anger: manage it with a system of rules, shifting its wrong-tracking function from the individual to society. Those who refuse to have their anger managed in this way are stigmatized as irrational, maybe mad: undomesticated fury is unwelcome in the "civilized" world.[2]

Like the Greeks, those who speak of Black rage also do not believe that anger should fester in the heart. They also think anger should be addressed collectively. But in contrast to the Western paradigm, those who speak of Black rage do not see society's role as managing individual anger through objective rules and laws. Rather, Black rage calls into question the legitimacy of society's rules and laws. It calls us to imagine collective life otherwise. Put another way, anger might not mark a discrete wrong, a failure to follow a certain social norm; it might mark a whole set of social norms as wrong. This deeper sense of anger deserves a stronger name: rage. Because rage points to such a sweeping wrong, it is felt not individually but collectively, by all those subject to a wrong set of social norms. When rage is voiced, it evokes solidarity rather than sympathy. Witnessing rage draws out our intuitions that we are subject to unjust social norms, that we too are subject to domination and want to be free.

Yet as a second-order anger, rage is subject to confusion just like first-order anger. We are enraged at situations that do not call for it, or not enraged when we ought to be. We can also confuse the orders of anger, feeling as if a whole set of rules and laws is wrong when in fact only one discrete wrong has been committed, one norm has been broken—or perhaps we misperceived and there was no wrong at all. All youth culture, all the social norms that hold young people's worlds together, can be condemned for the transgressively loud music of one youth, which might not even constitute a wrong. Rage in its purest form implicates us: we participate in and are invested in (in some senses are constituted by) the sets of social norms at which we rage. In its purest form, rage leaves us mute, as our very words are implicated in the sets of norms it condemns. Or nearly mute: in those media that themselves habitually transgress social norms, such as music, song, poetry, and prayer, rage finds its voice.

Furthermore, rage is always muffled and masked. The normative worlds it calls into question do not want their wrongness exposed. For patriarchy to survive, it must quiet women's rage. Women must be taught that voicing rage is inappropriate, the product of a bad personality, or madness, or hormones. The truth-speaking that rage entails must be silenced, and then the system of domination that is patriarchy can be naturalized—*mutatis mutandis* for the silenced rage of those with disabilities, transgender folks, those who are incarcerated, and those in the working class. Or rage can be offered a place in the world against which it rebels: for example, a populist leader claiming to reflect a people's rage but actually containing it, channeling it, using it to feed his own interests or the interests of the system of domination that he represents. But of course, real rage is still there: the soul is wounded but not destroyed. Rage bubbles up in unexpected places. When it does, it looks like evidence of madness, unconnected to any identifiable wrong. That is precisely the point: there is something so wrong with the world that classes of people, those subject to domination, are unable to give voice to the wrongs they face.

Black rage names rage directed at anti-Blackness, at a regime of racial domination. Anti-Blackness pervades the world; we suffer from it especially in the United States. Every attempt to express Black rage is compromised; hence the need to resort to genres other than the expository. When Black rage bubbles up, it is often dismissed as a defective personality, *angry Black woman*, or as pathological, in need of correction by the state or by vigilantes. But sometimes an expression of Black rage catches, echoes, calls forth the concealed rage of others— and so begins to take shape. It is only collectively that rage refines itself and gains confidence. What rage looks like when it takes shape is collective struggle aimed at ending domination, whether that struggle is through art, organizing, or imagining otherwise. Struggle against domination is dignity, and rage animates it. No rage, no dignity.

Another name for rage is righteous indignation, and Nick Bromell has persuasively argued that indignation is at the heart of the Black political tradition. How can rage accompany dignity if it names indignity? Rage given shape through collective action names the performance of dignity. Indignation is rage raw—rage at the treatment of a human as less than human. When that happens again and again, and when it happens to others, and when those who experience such indignity talk together and compare notes on the domination that gives rise to their indignation, then we find dignity. Dignity is impossible without indignity; indignity may become dignity. Because the world is chock-full of interlocking systems of domination, there will always be indignity—so there may always be dignity. But shaping indignation is a fraught process; those who benefit from domination have ideas about how it should be channeled that have nothing to do with dignity. False ideas of dignity proliferate, achieving a resemblance to dignity from their shared origin in indignation. Populist leaders promise dignity for working-class or Black people. Advocates of nonviolence promise dignity through channeling indignation into peaceful resistance, mislabeling that "struggle." In short, appreciation of Black rage goes wrong outside the framework of Black dignity.[3]

Martin Luther King, Jr., turned his indignation into disciplined, peaceful protest, keeping his cool and modeling for his followers how to face off against angry white police officers and mobs—at least, this is how we remember him. There were certainly times when he spoke or wrote in conformity with this image. As the Black power movement was emerging in the last years of his life, King sympathized with the impatient, indignant youths marching under that banner, but he cautioned that racial justice would be more quickly achieved if activists embraced a calmer and more disciplined mood. From King's perspective, Malcolm X and Stokely Carmichael were channeling Black rage in counterproductive directions. They were urging Blacks toward self-destruction, evidenced by the urban uprisings of the 1960s that would only accelerate after King's death. King's method, "nonviolent resistance," would not result in "explosions of anger": instead "it controlled anger and released it under discipline for maximum effect." He described this approach as "healthy," unlike that of his opponents, which set Blacks on a course "so desperate that it ends in black suicide." King's opponents encouraged Blacks to parrot the words and deeds of angry whites—but only the whites have power, and such an asymmetric conflict could only accelerate Black death. In King's assessment, the campaigns he led offered "a way to transmute the inchoate rage of the ghetto into a constructive and creative channel."[4]

This is the disciplined, gently disciplining side of King that was remembered and sanctified by multiculturalism. In recent years, Black critics have held up another side. Sometimes they have focused on the "radical" King who, in his later years, spoke out against the Vietnam War and U.S. imperialism despite what it cost him politically. From this perspective, it looks as though King's anger finally overtook his discipline as his public interventions veered away from the civil rights struggle in the United States toward broader issues that would endanger the coalition he had built. Other commentators suggest that King's most famous texts, such as the letter from Birmingham City Jail, show clearly that he was motivated by Black rage. As Mychal Denzel Smith puts it, "You cannot read or hear him without feeling that palpable sense of frustration, fury, and anger." Smith believes King was motivated by an "impatience born of rage." King knew that white people, even white liberals, were made uncomfortable by Black rage, so he emphasized nonviolence and discipline, but at the end of the day, his rage was unmistakable.[5]

At one level, the cautious King was right: unfettered expressions of Black rage led to violence, Black death, and few public policy gains for racial justice. But short-term pragmatism may not be the appropriate framework for evaluating modes of political organizing and rhetoric. This is all the more true given the violence and death that already afflicted the Black community. If the late 1960s and early 1970s were characterized by public expressions of Black rage—always a paradoxical endeavor given the anti-Black contamination of modes of expression—the three-plus decades that followed, the era of multiculturalism, nearly erased Black rage from public view. When it became visible, as in the language of Louis Farrakhan and Angela Davis, it was dismissed as kooky, cordoned off as dangerous, or categorized as a vestige of a bygone era.

One notable exception was the feminist critic bell hooks. Her pacific public persona and intellectual journey from Marxism to Buddhist and New Age thought allowed her cutting reflections on Black rage in the mid-1990s to see print, though at that point the ideology of multiculturalism was so strong that hooks remained identified with a rather saccharine love ethic, not as a proponent of anger. In the lead essay of her 1995 book *Killing Rage*, hooks samples her own encounters with racial discrimination and concludes that rage is an emotion that unites the Black community. "Sharing rage connects those of us who are older and more experienced with younger black and non-black folks who are seeking ways to be self-actualized, self-determined, who are eager to participate in anti-racist struggle."[6]

As a product and champion of the era of multiculturalism, hooks believed it was a time when Blacks could finally express the rage they had been prohibited from expressing during the era of segregation, on pain of bodily violence or death. Blacks of all stripes from the North and South could now bond with each other by sharing experiences of rage. But she also recognized that multiculturalism brought new incentives to dampen Black rage. Many Black people's career prospects, for instance, depended on "good" Black behavior, which meant never showing anger. hooks writes in the genre of exhortation: she asks her Black readers to take the risk of embracing their rage even as that embrace costs them opportunities and distances them from their peers who desire success in the white world. The payoff for embracing rage was a deep sense of connection with fellow Blacks, as well as the potential for rage to fuel creative world-building for Blacks beyond the limits set by the white status quo. She did not anticipate that the very act of revealing Black feeling was precisely what the new multicultural status quo desired. Black feeling, whether love or hope or indignation, would interestingly adorn Blacks in the multicultural pantheon, together with soul food and dashikis.

In 2011, during the last days of multiculturalism's reign, the journalist Ellis Cose published *The End of Anger: A New Generation's Take on Race and Rage.* According to Cose, the election of Barack Obama had made Black rage a thing of the past. Black Americans were optimistic about their and the nation's future. During the 2008 election, America had glimpsed residual Black anger in the form of Obama's former pastor, Jeremiah Wright, whose angry words "God damn America!" were replayed across the nation. Obama had mastered the soothing rhetoric of the multicultural era: "For the men and women of Reverend Wright's generation, the memories of humiliation and doubt and fear have not gone away; nor has the anger and the bitterness of those years." These angry older Blacks, Obama explained, do not express their anger in front of whites—hence the surprise with which white America encountered Wright—but the anger persists. "At times, that anger is exploited by politicians, to gin up votes along racial lines, or to make up for a politician's own failings." Obama implicitly assured his listeners that he was not that sort of politician. He was of a different generation, one that came of age in freedom and never had occasion to rage. His disposition was so steady, so free from anger, that the comedian Keegan-Michael Key could get easy laughs playing the president's "anger translator."[7]

In a pair of articles titled "The Function of Black Rage" (2014) and "The Rebirth of Black Rage" (2015), Mychal Denzel Smith analyzes how the place of rage in Black culture changed so quickly. On his account, the shift started even before Obama's election. Black anger began to regain visibility in 2005, when Kanye West went off script at a fundraiser for victims of Hurricane Katrina and proclaimed "George Bush doesn't care about Black people." The next year, Black youths across the country made their outrage known at the conviction of the Jena Six, a group of Black teenagers in Louisiana accused of beating a white classmate. When Obama was elected, Smith suggests, Black youths associated him with their parents, whom they saw as excessively invested in respectability. The protests against police violence triggered by the deaths of Trayvon Martin and Michael Brown, largely led by Black youths, gave this sentiment public visibility, and Ta-Nehisi Coates's 2015 book *Between the World and Me* promised an intellectual account of Black rage. Black rage was back, and multiculturalism was over.[8]

Despite the public invisibility of Black rage during the era of multiculturalism, in radical feminist circles rage was continually embraced and theorized. hooks's brief attempt to translate the insights of this tradition for a broader audience fell flat; after *Killing Rage,* she went back to writing about the power of love. The touchstone of radical feminist discussions of rage is the Black writer Audre Lorde's 1981 essay "The Uses of Anger." Along with Assata Shakur and Octavia Butler, Lorde has become one of the patron saints of today's racial justice movement, and her essay on anger is something like a sacred text. While the Christian moral vision—and by extension America's Christian-influenced moral vision—numbers anger among the vices,

Lorde attempts a reversal. For her, anger is dismissed as a vice by defenders of the status quo precisely to take away a tool from those who would challenge the status quo.[9]

A subtle thinker and a careful writer, Lorde is after more than simple reversal. She offers a phenomenology of anger from the perspective of those struggling against domination. What matters for her is not so much anger itself but what happens when anger begins to take shape as collective action. This is a "painful process," she notes, but it is also illuminating. As I mobilize for action with those who share my rage, those around me are forced to make a choice. Are they with me or against me? Which is to say, are they victims of domination or do they dominate? Independent of what follows, this clarity about where people stand with respect to domination is valuable knowledge for the struggle. And it authorizes us to properly direct our other emotions. We are rightly frustrated and saddened by those who we know share in our struggle but who perceive it differently from how we do. Those who do not struggle but who dominate treat us with hatred and warrant no affection.[10]

First, Lorde urges, we must attend to our emotions, and then we must shape them. In contrast to King's metaphor, for Lorde, shaping emotions is not disciplining them. That would be an attempt to dominate ourselves, and it would inevitably fail. Lorde's preferred analogy is the "symphony" versus a "cacophony," and shaping emotions symphonically is something with which Black women have had a great deal of experience. Given the huge number of grave wrongs to be angry about, and the penalties for Black anger, Black women "have had to learn to orchestrate those furies so that they do not tear us apart," "have had to learn to move through them and use them for strength and force and insight within our daily lives." Black women do not need a charismatic leader to teach them how to be properly angry. They have anger, know their anger, and effectively channel their anger for survival. This is essential knowledge for struggle. As Black women talk collectively about the domination they face and the way anger can be harnessed, they develop a tool for struggle that could be invincible. Just as important, anger helps us imagine a world after struggle, a world without domination, a world where those who face domination are no longer divided against each other, and "where our children can love." Lorde is careful to distinguish today's world of struggle from this world of milk and honey existing on an eschatological horizon.[11]

In the years since Lorde wrote, feminist theorists have refined and expanded on her account of anger. Sara Ahmed sees the political project of feminism in moving "from anger into an interpretation of that which one is against, whereby associations or connections are made between the object of anger and broader patterns or structures." Tapping anger for survival may be familiar to women, particularly Black women, but political organizing can provide scaffolding to demonstrate that, with collective work, they can hope for more than mere survival. One person's causes of anger belong to the same system as another's causes of anger. The political work of explicating that system is guided by and also guides anger: it conducts the symphony.[12]

The Argentinian feminist María Lugones develops Lorde's account of anger's exclusion from the world and finds political potential in that exclusion. From the perspective of those who are well acculturated in the world, the anger of those experiencing domination fails to communicate. The words that express it sound irrational, and actions make an angry person seem possessed. Only the anger of those who dominate, used in the service of domination, communicates: it keeps people in their places. For Lugones, political education involves differentiating these two types of anger and reacting appropriately. The anger of those who dominate ought to be ignored. The concrete harms it causes should be mitigated matter-of-factly. In contrast, the anger of those who experience domination pulls those who are angry, and whose anger is rejected by those around them, toward another world—if only they can trust in their own anger. In that alternative world, the angry person is the one who has sense; the rest of the world is senseless. Such anger is not directed at this or that wrong, although it may be occasioned by a particular event. The anger of which Lugones writes is second-order anger, rage directed at the world as such insofar as the world is infected by domination. While this "separatist anger" is illegible from the world's perspective, when one person who experiences that rage encounters another such person, and another, and another, their rage "echoes across different worlds of sense," opening the way for coalitions of those who each experience domination in different ways and are deprived, individually, of the language to name the domination they endure.[13]

In the writing of today's racial justice activists, rage takes center stage. Author-activists model what it looks like to turn rage into a symphony, using this process to define the narrative arc of their lives. Austin Channing Brown includes a chapter in her memoir titled "Creative Anger," and she describes reading Lorde's "The Uses of Anger" as the turning point in her life, the moment she decided to self-consciously attend to her own anger. She realized that as a Black woman, she was afraid to be angry, but she found it difficult to keep calm given the anti-Blackness she continually encountered. Even as she began speaking out about racial justice, Brown would avoid anger, instead showing her audience her pain or her sadness. Aided by Lorde, Brown realized that she had to do work on herself to stop caring so much about how the white-dominated world judged her. This loosed her creativity, and she grew more effective at "proclaiming the human dignity of Black bodies." She became capable of writing a memoir titled *I'm Still Here: Black Dignity in a World Made for Whiteness.*[14]

The queer Black author-activist Darnell Moore also organized his memoir around grappling with rage. He recounts the rage felt by the Black community in Camden, New Jersey, during the late 1960s and early 1970s, and how it continued to affect individual lives when Moore was coming of age there in the 1980s. He retrospectively diagnoses a childhood bully who tormented him as suffering from this rage, born of poverty and violence. Moore himself felt the same rage as he grew to adulthood while enduring poverty, violence, and a fatherless home. "Anger suited me well," he writes. "I summoned my rage as a form of protection." It was "the only weapon I had mastered." In 2014 he felt the same rage while watching countless videos of the Ferguson protests. He discovered his friends were feeling it, too, and they organized a caravan to Ferguson to join the protests. Moore writes, "We had grown tired of containing our rage. We needed to release it." In collective organizing, in struggle against racial domination, he was able to shape his rage and make it manageable— and give meaning to his life.[15]

The Black feminist critic Brittney Cooper, inspired by Lorde, titled her memoir *Eloquent Rage: A Black Feminist Discovers Her Superpower*. Cooper writes that the behavior of Black women that is often labeled "sassy" is actually an expression of Black rage, masked to make it socially acceptable. Cooper's project for herself, and her invitation to readers, is to allow rage to shine through. She allows that rage can become eloquent in performance rather than language: she cites Venus and Serena Williams as expressing Black rage in active form. Rage can also be channeled into refusal to participate in the rituals of a white supremacist nation. (On this, she cites Michelle Obama's unkempt hair during Donald Trump's inauguration.) It can also be found writ small, in a curse uttered at what seems like an annoyance but is actually one facet of a seemingly indestructible system of domination.[16]

Black rage can build movements; according to Cooper, it built the Black Lives Matter movement. Once we collectively attend to the uncomfortable truths it reveals, we are moved to act together against those parts of the world that are built on lies. This is in sharp contrast to white rage (of the sort found in "Karens") which, according to Cooper, is a product of lies and serves to maintain them, along with the violence that accompanies them. The people best suited to discern rage oriented to truth from rage oriented to lies, she writes, are Black women, whose clarity of judgment comes from enduring patriarchy and anti-Blackness. To survive, Black women have had to think sharply and act quickly: "We know what it means to snatch dignity from the jaws of power and come out standing."[17]

For Cooper, rage and dignity are tightly connected. Her memoir is about rage; her other book, *Beyond Respectability,* an intellectual history of Black women activists, is about dignity. In the latter book she sets out to cleave dignity from respectability, which she does in part by attending to the rage that animates Black women's performances of dignity. Even though Black women often had to conceal this rage behind a mask of respectability, it was still there, and she argues that framing the story of Black women intellectuals in terms of respectability misses the mark. For example, describing the life and work of Mary Church Terrell, a late nineteenth-century educator and activist who co-founded and led the National Association of Colored Women, Cooper concludes, "Terrell's life fully inhabits the paradigm of respectable race womanhood. At the same time, she also mischievously and defiantly exceeds the frame of respectability politics." Her life's work was "dignified agitation."[18]

For Cooper, an activist and historian, there remains some fuzziness in what dignity really means. She often writes as if Black women were motivated by a realization that "dignity" names a quality all humans share simply by being human. "Dignity," she writes, "unlike respectability, is not socially contingent. It is intrinsic." This formulation sounds suspiciously like the European Christian tradition of understanding dignity as the inherent worth of each human being, in need of protection by international law. Why not find dignity performed in the "dignified agitation" of Mary Church Terrell—leaving respectability to signify a hollow status performed by some and then projected onto all?[19]

3

Black Love

In the late 1960s and early '70s, the Black power movement pivoted away from the language of love. It didn't seem effective. Militant youths from the Student Nonviolent Coordinating Committee and later the Black Panther Party took their lead instead from Malcolm X. Having renounced Christianity, Malcolm also rejected the vestigial Christian language contaminating political analysis. "Let us practice brotherhood among ourselves," he wrote, "and then if others want to practice brotherhood with us, we're for practicing it with them also. But I don't think we should run around trying to love somebody who doesn't love us." Black folks were being insulted, injured, and killed every day, and the perpetrators of these crimes deserved hatred, not love. What the nation (and the world) needed was a Black revolution, and revolutions involve enmity, not amity. This vision lost its appeal during the decades of multiculturalism at the end of the twentieth century and the start of the twenty-first. Love-of-enemy came to be seen as the particular gift of Black people, an exemplary testimony to our virtue given the innumerable hardships we have endured.[1]

On the surface, it looks as though today's new racial justice movement follows Martin Luther King rather than Malcolm. The language of love is all over the movement. It began with love. Following George Zimmerman's acquittal, Alicia Garza posted a "love letter to Black people" on her Facebook wall: "Black people. I love you. I love us. Our lives matter," to which her friend Patrisse Cullors responded, "#blacklivesmatter," bringing the hashtag into being. During the movement's peak years, Garza used the provocatively ambiguous Twitter handle "Love God Herself." On Martin Luther King, Jr., Day in 2015, Tometi, Garza, and Cullors posted an appreciation of King's legacy: "Dr. King nurtured visions of a movement that could restore a deep and abiding love for all of humanity." They found this commitment inspiring even as they saw the Black Lives Matter movement "innovating on its strategies, practices, and approaches," with particular attention to including, and centering, the most marginalized—making sure love was truly directed at *all* humanity.[2]

One of the most robust local groups organizing under the Black Lives Matter banner, Chicago-based Black Youth Project 100, lists "holistic energy" among its core values. By this it means "We bring our entire selves to the work. Our efforts are driven by love." BYP100 puts an emphasis on cultural work as political work: by cultivating a sense of self-worth and communal connection artists and musicians can generate Black love. Its founding director, Charlene Carruthers, recognizes the power love can have in organizing communities of the vulnerable, whose lives are filled with anxiety. In such contexts, love is an essential part of a "powerful chemistry" that ignites and accelerates movements for radical transformation. In 2016, the activist Dante Barry, who led the organization Million Hoodies for Justice, wrote an article for *Ebony* in which he made the case for love as a "revolutionary act" essential for today's racial justice movement. He argued, "The ability to love each other is our people's secret weapon in this war against the Black body, and that is revolutionary. Revolutionary love is the ability to risk it all for the love of our people." Racial domination, in his analysis, survives on devaluing Black lives and Black bodies. To love Black lives and Black bodies is to challenge racial domination, to throw a wrench in its workings. Blacks who are loved realize immediately that we do not deserve to be degraded and stand ready to challenge those who would degrade us.[3]

The love that circulates as part of the new racial justice vocabulary is importantly distinct from the love practiced in the caricatured civil rights movement. The sense of love embraced by activists, commentators, and ordinary Black youths today is not saccharine, and it is racially specific. It is *Black love*. Malcolm's commitment to Black brotherhood is built into its definition. It refuses to be domesticated by multiculturalism, and it is wed to dignity. Black love is how it feels to struggle together against racial domination, whether that struggle manifests at a protest or in daily life—or in intimate encounters. As Black feminists so powerfully argue, domination contaminates even the bodily and erotic realms. But so does struggle: dignity is nourished by the unique power of self-love and bodily encounter.

The Black feminist insistence on love's bodily and erotic dimensions adds a crucial element that was missing from the thought of Malcolm X and King. But it also makes talk of Black love vulnerable to co-optation by multiculturalism, and to the economic forces with which multiculturalism is always entangled. The *Blackness* of Black love can slip away—precisely when Black love loses its attachment to struggle, and to dignity. We need critical tools to identify love detached from dignity, love's false copies. Only then can we rightly appreciate love's power. I suggest that we return to King's reflections on love with new eyes, focusing on his challenge to false loves rather than his imperative to love. This focus on the negative (on struggle, on dignity) is a through line from King to Black power leaders, whose best insights into Black love's positive dimensions resonate with the Black feminist tradition and the Black Lives Matter movement today.

The era of multiculturalism was anchored by a particular way of remembering King: as a prophet of love. He was not only a political organizer but a Christian minister, and love was at the heart of his message. Often, the love of which he spoke so eloquently is imagined to be colorblind. His message is flattened to an exhortation for all Americans to love each other more. There are people who would hate; they must be converted to love, by means of love. Such love is unconditional. Each human being deserves to be loved, and when we are our best selves, we love each human we encounter. Laws may change, but there is still an imperative to convert hearts to the side of love. All this is right, but it is only part of the story. Today it is hard to hear what King said about love because, in the intervening years, love talk proliferated until it was void of nearly all meaning. This process began before King's death. The summer of 1967 was the "Summer of Love," the same summer the Beatles released "All You Need is Love." With love, the Beatles sang to their adoring fans, everything is possible, everything can be known, and everyone can find their place. As the limited lyrics ("All you need is love" repeated twelve times, "Love is all you need" repeated twenty-four times) suggest, love offers a simple solution for a world full of ills: "It's easy," they exclaim.[4]

For King, love was not easy. In his speeches and writings, he has very little of substance to say about what love is, and much more developed views about what it is not. Our lives are full of what seem like feelings of love but are actually false copies of love. We lust after "gadgets and contrivances," "television," and "luxurious cars." We make these into "little gods" that we worship, that order our loves. We also make abstractions into little gods: science, nationalism, wealth. For a time, King offered Sunday morning radio broadcasts dedicated to "False Gods We Worship," taking up one idol each week to assure us that all the objects and ideas he condemns will ultimately disappoint us—or worse. Love of science can lead to nuclear annihilation, love of nation can lead to senseless war, and love of money can lead us to stop enjoying life as we pursue wealth.[5]

But what, for King, is love? To speak rightly about such an ultimate concern, he advises, we should be wary of "philosophical and theological categories" and instead listen to "old people" who speak in a "poetic manner." If we try to give an account of the necessary and sufficient conditions for love, we will get it wrong. We will reduce love to the terms of the world, and the world is infected by domination. What the philosopher or theologian can do is clear away worldly ideas that block us from loving. In this way, we can vehemently condemn injustice (or domination) without hatred, for injustice blocks love. King quotes the theologian Paul Tillich: "Condemnation is not the negation of love but the negation of the negation of love." If there were no injustice in the world, if every system of domination were dismantled, love would flow effortlessly everywhere. But that is not our world. It may be inspirational to conjure that world—employing the "poetic manner" of "old people" rather than logic—but for purposes of political and ethical analysis and action, we should focus on attacking love's simulacra. This is precisely how King framed the Montgomery bus boycott at the first mass meeting after the boycott was called: "Justice is love correcting that which revolts against love."[6]

When we confront systems of domination, King says, we are tempted to accede to them, or to hate. The problem with hatred, and what distinguishes it from vehement condemnation, is that it tends to affix to individuals rather than systems, and in doing so it tends to psychically damage the one who hates: it "scars the soul." When we hate anyone, it becomes harder and harder to love freedom, and so to rightly calibrate our actions to best dismantle systems of domination. The humanity of one who is hated is not exhausted by his participation in systems of domination. In this world, no one is entirely master or entirely slave. We all participate in systems of domination, and it is to those systems that our ire must be directed.[7]

When we refuse to accede to domination and we reject hatred, we open ourselves to love. Even then it is easy to be misled. We tend to model the love that is called for on romantic love (with all its "emotional bosh") or on friendship. But for King, love in its truest sense is something more. It is tempting to turn to the Good Samaritan's "love," understood as the imperative to help a stranger in need. But according to King, if you happen upon a traveler stripped and beaten beside the road, the loving response is not only to aid the victim but to "clear this Jericho road of its robbers." What genuine love looks like, in this world of domination, is when you "tear down unjust conditions and build anew instead of patching things up." Such love does not happen alone: it requires collective action, organization. In that action, that organizing, love resides. Moreover, that collective action must be guided by an understanding of how pervasive domination is in the world. Recognizing this fact allows King to separate his position from what he describes as the position of Communists. Communists, he suggests, instrumentalize human lives in order to end domination, but in the process they enact a new domination. In King's view, we must never forget that love is directed toward freedom for all, including those white folks whose lives are clouded by their participation in toxic dynamics of racial domination that they do not even recognize. Deep down, they too have an intuition that they endure domination, and if this intuition can be activated, however unlikely that seems, they can be enlisted in the struggle. They can participate in love. The more clearly struggle is directed against systems of domination rather than individuals, the more likely it is that the instincts of even one's apparent enemies, even those playing the role of slave master, will be activated: this is love's promise.[8]

To understand Black love, we must begin with the primal scene of racial domination: white master and Black slave. No love can flow from master to slave in this scene, no matter how kind the master purports to be or how rarely or gently he imposes his will upon the slave. Any affection the master feels for the slave is nullified by his acting as if the slave were not actually a human being. An essential element of love is attending rightly to the beloved. Love names that feeling that compels us to attend: to look again and again, ever more carefully, patiently, at our object of love. The book, painting, land, or man or woman we love draws our attention over and over, and we are ever surprised by the novelty of what we notice. Misperception leads to false feeling: the master may believe he loves his slave, but what he feels is a false copy of love. (Incidentally, two masters are unable to genuinely love each other as well, for their self-understanding as masters depends on a misperception of both themselves and the one they purport to love.) What the master mistakes for love could be lust fueled by the desire for possession, always elusive when the object to be possessed is a human being. It could be self-satisfaction, the pleasure of fulfilling a fantasy of liberality. Or it could simply be comfort with the familiar; comfort and affection are easily confused. Whatever his true feeling, a master does not love his slave, although he may be quite invested in proclaiming this love and believing it exists.

Needless to say, a slave does not love her master, either. She may say she does, and may believe she does, but this too is a false copy of love. It may be comfort masquerading as love, but more likely it is the perverse affection that power elicits, whether it is held by a king, a boss, or a master. (Or a man.) It is as if associating my affections with one who is powerful grants me power. Of course it may: to be favored by the powerful can be highly advantageous. But the object of affection in such cases is the perceived power, not the person, and as the person is confused with his power, it seems as if he is loved. As Carruthers points out, this dynamic is put on steroids when a particularly vulnerable person (in this case, one enslaved) encounters the powerful (the master). Hence it is not surprising to find slaves expressing affection for their masters, but this does not qualify as love, and most often the affection is only a thin veneer. Recall the grand lesson Ralph Ellison's

invisible protagonist learns from his grandfather: "I want you to overcome 'em with yeses, undermine 'em with grins, agree 'em to death
and destruction, let 'em swoller you till they vomit or bust wide open."[9]

What does a slave love? Nothing in the world of slavery. Everything, every place, every person, is shadowed by the condition of en-
slavement. The only thing a slave loves is freedom. In this case,
freedom is not an abstraction; abstractions cannot be loved. Freedom
means specific people and places as they would be, free of domination. A slave loves herself as she would be, free of domination. She
loves her fellows as they would be, free of domination. She loves her
land as it would be, free of domination. (She still does not love her
master, for her master is inextricable from domination.) She knows
that domination distorts personalities, including her own, and dis-
tends the land. She also knows that domination does not have the last
word, that she is not who her master says she is—even if she may not
have the words to articulate it. This true love of freedom motivates
her to struggle in small ways, and perhaps to realize a kind of freedom:
to struggle against her master, to struggle against domination. When
the struggle takes on collective form, those who struggle together are
bound by their shared love of freedom, including for each other as
free. For the enslaved, love, like rage, fuels struggle, and that struggle
is properly named dignity. As Patrisse Cullors puts it, "When we show
up on the freeway, when we chain ourselves to each other, that's an act
of love. That act of resistance is an act of love."[10]

From the primal scene of domination we can move downstream to
subtler contexts, times when domination conceals itself in systems and
laws and habits—without losing any of its malevolence. To understand
Black love, which is to understand all genuine love, we must route our
analysis through slavery. The love that those who comfortably inhabit
systems of domination purport to have for those who feel the full force
of domination is false love. King rightly urges us to cast a suspicious eye

on the white liberal, on those whites who most loudly proclaim their love for Blacks. The love that some of those subject to domination purport to have for the things most associated with their own domination may also prove a false love (a point Christian theologians have been making since Augustine). The pompous Black intellectual's purported love for opera or John Dewey or golf, or a white wife, may fall into this category if it is disordered by domination. Black love is love aimed at getting free. It is love for self and others and home and land as they would be when they are free. It is love that fuels struggle for that freedom, struggle against the forces of racial domination that stand in the way of that freedom. Given that our actual messy world is never free from domination and that freedom resides on an eschatological horizon, the purest form of love that we can find in our world is love that grows in struggle, love of those who struggle together in order to get free. A shared vision of domination and orientation in struggle is the prerequisite for Black love. If Black love names bonds of brotherhood and sisterhood, the family it constitutes is not based on skin color or African ancestry but on struggling together against racial domination.

To map domination in its primal scene of slavery onto today's world is an essential task, but it encounters a great many complications. In the real world, where there are innumerable interlocking systems of domination, racial domination is just one particularly malignant species. Even if we imagine we could separate racial domination from other forms, there is not a discrete set of masters administering that domination but a whole race of people, whites, together with other races (treated at times as honorary whites), together with institutions and laws and habits and symbols and words that all together make up the system of racial domination, downstream from the primal scene of slavery. Complexity does not mean impossibility: we need not give up on routing analysis through slavery. The world gives us clues. Among them are rage and love. As with any clue, their meaning is not self-evident; even their existence is not self-evident. They require careful attention, and the more we collectively attend to them, the more precise their guidance becomes. For rage, attending often involves noticing and appreciating rage that was once hidden or dismissed as impermissible. For love, attending often involves telling apart love from its simulacra, for in our world today proclamations of love are over-abundant. Discerning Black love is a goal of this mapping process, but it also facilitates the process. Black love requires shared commitment to struggle, and part of that struggle is a struggle against the domination within our own psyches that distorts our judgment and draws us toward what we think is love when we are really attracted by lust, comfort, self-satisfaction, or power.

But Black love does not only entail labor on the self. It also involves intense feeling, commitment, habit, and joy. It can titillate and frustrate. It offers strength and requires us to risk heartbreak. This all happens in the intense connections forged through struggling together against domination's many tentacles. Those who share in struggle turn out to be disloyal, successes turn to failures and failures to successes, and the promise of victory is sweet while setbacks are wrenching. But we should not think too much of romance. Where romantic love has become the model of all love (of friends, family, and God) in white America, Black love takes as its paradigm the mutual love of comrades in struggle. To be comrades in struggle requires discipline, reliability, habits of attention and perseverance, commitment in the face of difficulty, and affection. Where white America subtracts components from romantic love to apply the concept of love elsewhere, Black love for close friends, family, partners, and home has the same shape as comradely love but greater intensity. As we will see, for George Jackson and Eldridge Cleaver, even romantic love has as its prerequisite a shared orientation to struggle. Certainly it also has other components, and it gains intensity through intimacy, but if at any point the lovers did not share an understanding of anti-Black racism and a commitment to struggle against it, the love would go sour. If a relationship remained, it would be a false copy of love.[11]

Where there is Black dignity, there is Black love. Those who struggle against domination are motivated by love for freedom, for the free version of themselves; they also love those who share in their struggle. In the real world, these ideal types do not cleanly divide loves but guide judgment. We all struggle against domination in some ways; we all dominate others in some ways. Thus, all loves inevitably involve struggling together, and they also inevitably involve the hollow master's love characteristic of domination. When making judgments in the world about those with whom we wish to affiliate and those we wish to avoid or condemn, we attend to complex circumstances, along with known unknowns and unknown unknowns. But we must act and speak, and we must do so passionately, condemning and cutting off false loves, embracing Black love.

While the Black nationalist currents that overtook King's Christian activism in the 1960s were officially suspicious of love, in fact a cohort of Black power intellectuals did a great deal of work theorizing love. Two books that came to define the era for the general public, Eldridge Cleaver's *Soul on Ice* (1968) and George Jackson's *Soledad Brother* (1970), were in fact love stories—although most people read them as political tracts. The account of love, specifically Black love, that Cleaver and Jackson develop resonates strongly with the views articulated by movement leaders today. Cleaver and Jackson argue that Black love first requires a hard break from wrongly ordered loves, loves that are shaped by systems of domination, which they define as anti-Black racism and capitalism.[12]

Cleaver and Jackson were each incarcerated in California at the age of eighteen, Cleaver on a marijuana charge, Jackson for stealing

$70 from a gas station. Each came of age behind bars, read widely, reflected on his situation, and began writing. Each concluded that the American prison is a continuation of slavery and segregation, a system for controlling Black bodies and souls, and that American racism runs so deep that discrete public policy fixes will never be adequate. Only a radical reconfiguration of American society and economy could adequately address American racism: they called for revolution. Before a grand revolution, though, they called for a revolution of the heart. Each recalled how he had transformed his loves upon realizing the depths of anti-Black racism.

Cleaver's conversion began in the prison psychiatric ward. The psychiatrist wanted him to talk about his parents; Cleaver wanted to talk about racism. He self-diagnosed his mental health problems as rooted in racism. He had suffered a breakdown on seeing a picture of the white woman who was said to have flirted with fourteen-year-old Emmett Till, precipitating Till's widely publicized lynching. "While looking at this picture," Cleaver writes, "I felt that little tension in the center of my chest I experience when a woman appeals to me. I was disgusted and angry with myself." Two days later, his mental health was in total collapse. The photograph forced him to recognize just how disordered his loves were, and it was too much for him to handle.[13]

To recover, Cleaver had to come up with a story to explain how his loves were disordered; he had to theorize. He asserted that whiteness had become associated with the intellect, Blackness with physical labor. Because of this, white women were in the impossible position of having to reject all that is associated with the body; white men, who according to the racial order are supposed to desire white women, have this desire thwarted by white women's rejection of their own bodies. Black women embrace their bodies and desire social advancement and security, and so would naturally pair off with white men if it were not for the prohibition on miscegenation. Similarly, white women look to

Black men as an outlet for their repressed sensual desires. For Black men like himself, Cleaver feels, the situation is hopeless. They have been acculturated to think of Black women as merely physical, more animal than human. White women hold the promise of social advancement and serve as symbols of freedom, so desire for (and self-protective aversion from) white women pervade Black male life and love. For this reason, Cleaver considers the white woman demonic, her "claws buried in the core of my being, . . . like a cancer eating my heart out and devouring my brain." Cleaver is writing here about erotic love, but his diagnosis is broader: all Black loves have been disordered by the anti-Black world. He was, for example, "in love with" marijuana when he first went to prison. His prescription is broader, too: those tainted loves must be repudiated and new loves instilled.[14]

Jackson does not offer such an elaborate theory, but his conclusions are the same. Racial and economic domination "have reduced all life to a very dull formula," with the result that "all natural feelings have been lost." Those with power do not like surprises; surprises threaten their hold on power. The powerful create abstractions through which they seek to understand and thus order the world. Reason is sufficient to live in such a world; feeling is superfluous. Those with power forget about the real world, with its complications and mysteries and surprises. Blacks' love for other Blacks, romantic or otherwise, threatens to disrupt the capitalist, white supremacist order and so is discouraged, resulting in disordered Black loves.[15]

When Cleaver and Jackson realized their loves were disordered, at first they rebelled. As Cleaver puts it, "Any affirmative assertion made by anyone around me became a target for tirades and criticism and denunciation." Racist domination seemed ubiquitous and suffocating; his only option was to say no to everything and to lash out. But eventually he realized that this mood of pure negation left him under the sway of the racial order he wished to reject. Further analysis of world and self was necessary. "I had to seek out the truth and unravel the snarled web of my motivations." This analytic moment was possible only because of his earlier reaction to racist domination. Only after having spent time filled with hatred for that system of domination and all its components could he achieve clarity to unravel his own disordered loves.[16]

In contrast, Jackson purged his disordered desires through ascesis. In his prison cell, he took stock of what he loved and attempted to stamp out tainted love, both intellectually and physically, with calisthenics. As he proceeded, Jackson reported, "My mind is fast becoming clear and I am slowly harnessing my emotions." The new loves that he eventually allowed to fill the void he created were not based on abstractions but on concrete perception of things, people, and himself, ever deepening along with his attention. But he was in prison, and he knew the confines of his cell should not have the last word on his loves. "Believe me, there is a better life," he wrote. This is the principle that now ordered his loves: freedom, a love of himself and the world as it would be, free. Writ large, the name of this ordering principle is revolution. He aspired for his heart to be populated with love for revolution, and for his loves to be ordered by the principle of revolution— an aspiration he shared with Cleaver.[17]

Under California law, Jackson's sentence, originally one year, could be extended indefinitely if his behavior was seen as insubordinate— and it was. Freedom and revolution were clearly on an eschatological horizon, even as they acted as guides in the real world of his cell. Yet worldly loves, for Jackson, must still be ordered by this principle, even as the ordering can only be imperfect. "I feel no love, no tenderness, for anyone who does not think as I do," Jackson asserted, with what seems like egotism but is actually a call for comradeship. When he imagined romance, it was built on a shared willingness to sacrifice all worldly things "not solely because she loved me, but because she loved the principle, the revolution, the people." This might seem like another abstraction of the sort Jackson had purged, but in fact it is the opposite: the revolution names the world without dominating abstractions, the world free. His acclaimed book, *Soledad Brother*, is political analysis in the form of letters to those he loves, both family members and women. Political analysis and love became, for him, inextricable.[18]

Cleaver's political treatise takes the form of love letters to his white lawyer, Beverly Axelrod. Like Jackson's love, Cleaver's love for Axelrod is made possible by their shared orientation toward freedom. He describes Axelrod as "a revolutionary who is alienated fundamentally from the *status quo*, probably with as great an intensity, conviction, and irretrievability as I am alienated from it." It is ironic that Cleaver would direct romantic love to a white woman, but behind bars in 1960s America he was living in a pre-eschatological, pre-revolutionary world. What was non-negotiable was a shared analysis of domination and a shared orientation to struggle, but there was no purity to be found in a world pervaded by domination.[19]

Rather than propose an anodyne love ethic, King, Cleaver, and Jackson identified genuine love with the struggle against domination, aligning Black love with Black dignity. The Beatles, and the cultural shift they represented, helped us forget this meaning of love. Yet the focus on the negative found in these thinkers overlooks the sensuous, bodily dimension of love that Black feminists emphasize. In Alice Walker's 1982 novel *The Color Purple*, a runaway success that brought her the Pulitzer Prize and the National Book Award, the telos is love of self and other that is rooted in sensuality. She described that book as a "theological work examining the journey from the religious back to the spiritual." The protagonist, Celie, endures abuse and seeks salvation by worldly means as well as by writing to an absent God. Celie is able to flourish only when she comes to identify God with Spirit and nonjudgmental love, allowing her to embrace her own wounded body and soul along with the world around her. She is helped to this realization by Shug, the woman who teaches her that love is possible in the world, "warm and cushiony," "like heaven," or like the best sort of music, "the devil's," when "singing and dancing and fucking" join. In 1983, Walker published a brief manifesto defining Black feminism with a new label, "womanism." By this she meant "a woman who loves other women, sexually and/or nonsexually." A womanist "loves music. Loves dance. Loves the moon. *Loves* the Spirit. Loves love." With this repeated "love," Walker risks aligning herself more with the Beatles than with Martin Luther King, Jr. While she might take issue with the claim that love is "easy," it certainly seems to provide all the answers. At times it seems as though, for Walker, love is the opposite of struggle. We genuinely love when our love spreads out to the world, embracing all, condemning none.[20]

If Alice Walker draws attention to the centrality of love in Black life and proclaims that love nonjudgmental, Audre Lorde similarly centers love but puts greater emphasis on judgment. Walker was embraced by the era of multiculturalism, with *The Color Purple* elevated to canonical status, while Lorde remained a marginal figure, embraced primarily in radical feminist circles. Recently, this has changed, and Lorde's 1978 essay "The Uses of the Erotic," like her essay on rage, is a key text of the racial justice movement, informing how Black love is understood today. According to Lorde, love, like anger, is a resource we can access, one that women are particularly able to harness. Access to love, like access to anger, has been suppressed by those who dominate: whites and men. Love offers a taste of fulfillment, wholeness, and utter joy (for example, in orgasm) that is absent from the world, priming us to struggle for fulfillment that we are denied—and so to struggle against the forces that deny us. And love experienced with another models the sort of interpersonal exchange needed in any collective.[21]

Importantly, for Lorde, love promises access to truth but never fully grants it. Lovers must carefully attend to each other's feelings and bodies in order to achieve fulfillment, and that fulfillment is not eternal. More attention is necessary, and through such attention the lovers gain knowledge. Systems of domination mute or mask our access to our loves, or they separate intellectual, emotional, and bodily loves. The more we attend to our own loves, the more we repair the psychic harm—the wounds to the soul—that systems of domination have inflicted on us. Love necessarily involves judgment; otherwise we are controlled by false loves. Lorde agrees with King that we ought to negate the negation of love, but as for what remains after that double negation, King can give us only an eschatological promise: at the end of days, when the world is free from domination, all will love. (Only then will we live in Walker's world of overflowing, undirected love.) Lorde argues that we can have a foretaste of this eschatological sense of love in our present world, in the bodily, emotional, and intellectual satisfaction we can experience with those we love. Yet Lorde shares King's negative impulse: she always emphasizes how provisional and limited these foretastes are. They motivate, but they call for discernment. For King, in contrast, our only foretaste of true love is in the biblical accounts of Jesus.

The powerful, sensuous account of love put forward by Black feminists converges with the critique of false loves put forward by King, Cleaver, and Jackson in the writings of Assata Shakur. While Cleaver and Jackson are not central figures of the Black Lives Matter pantheon, Shakur is deeply revered. Like Cleaver and Jackson, she spent time in the Black Panther Party and was committed to revolutionary struggle. In the early 1970s, in the face of nationwide police crackdowns on Black nationalist movements, Shakur went underground. In 1973 she was arrested following a shootout with New Jersey state police that left an officer wounded. In 1979 she escaped from prison and now resides in Cuba. From there, she published her autobiography, a story of the ordering of her loves—critical and sensual, maternal and erotic, political and personal. As Audre Lorde puts it in a poem dedicated to the then-imprisoned Shakur, "Your smile has been to war."[22]

While on the run, Shakur made an audio recording to explain herself, written "in the spirit" of George Jackson and other victims of state violence whom she names. It begins, "Black brothers, Black sisters, I want you to know that I love you and I hope that somewhere in your hearts you have love for me." Recall Alicia Garza's founding words of Black Lives Matter: "Black people. I love you. I love us. Our lives matter." When Garza recounts the history of the movement, she points to Shakur's message as an inspiration, though she does not mention the radical turn away from the world of racial and economic domination that Shakur calls for: "I am a revolutionary. A Black revolutionary. By that I mean that I have declared war on all forces that have raped our women, castrated our men, and kept our babies empty-bellied." Shakur asserts that because of her revolutionary stance, "America is trying to lynch me." But this stance is bound together with love, and with love Shakur's message opens and closes. Its final lines were picked up by many Black Lives Matter groups and recited as a kind of closing prayer:

> It is our duty to fight for our freedom.
> It is our duty to win.
> We must love each other and support each other.
> We have nothing to lose but our chains.[23]

4

Black Family

Phillip Jackson, a Black community activist in Chicago, said in 2007, "Father absence in the African American communities, across America, has hit those communities with the force of 100 Hurricane Katrinas." The next year, Senator Barack Obama echoed these sentiments to a Black church while campaigning for the presidency: "Too many fathers are M.I.A., too many fathers are AWOL, missing from too many lives and too many homes, acting like boys instead of men." Speaking on Father's Day, Obama exhorted Black men to take responsibility. Instead of sitting around watching sports on television, they should get involved in their kids' lives. Obama's comments echoed those made a few years earlier by Bill Cosby, who thrust anxieties about Black fatherhood into the national spotlight at an NAACP event commemorating the fiftieth anniversary of *Brown v. Board of Education*. According to Cosby, the end of legal segregation had shifted the burden to Black communities to fix their own problems: first and foremost, at the root of violence and incarceration, were absent Black fathers. "No longer," Cosby moralized, "is a boy considered an embarrassment if he tries to run away from being the father [of a] child."[1]

In the era of multiculturalism, the Black family was taken to be a problem. We could no longer blame discriminatory laws; now individuals were to blame. If only Blacks would act responsibly, we could flourish in this land of opportunity just like those family-focused

Asians, Jews, and Italians. For an earlier generation, Senator Daniel
Patrick Moynihan's 1965 report on the "Negro family" had codified
white liberals' fascination with supposed Black sexual deviance by ar-
guing that pervasive sex outside of marriage led to economic and social hardships in the Black community. Then, in the era of
multiculturalism, Black public figures took it upon themselves to
point out that Black families do not look like white families, and to
diagnose that as a problem. Moralizing about the "traditional" Black
family and the shortcomings of the modern Black family was a cornerstone of respectability politics. It was seldom mentioned that
nearly a million Black men were being held in cages and many more
were touched by the criminal justice system, keeping them unem-
ployable and pulling them away from their loved ones. Black families
looked different because of state violence, because of the afterlives of
slavery.[2]

Young activists today do not lament the deficiencies of the Black
family but instead redefine it. The model family is no longer the
white, patriarchal paradigm of a male-headed nuclear family. Rather,
family names those bound by love born of shared struggle. Influenced
in part by queer cultures' efforts to complicate the meaning of family,
Black family has taken on a porous meaning. Fatherhood does not
define it, and even the terms *brotherhood* and *sisterhood*, embraced by
earlier generations of activists, are tainted by the suggestion of gender-
norming. Black family instead suggests two components: one
positive, affection between comrades, and one negative, denial of the
patriarchal domination that is often entwined with racial domination. Thus redefined, Black family recovers a centuries-old tradition
of fluid Black intimacy and suspicion of male privilege that is concealed when respectability is the organizing framework. Instead of
seeing the relative lack of nuclear families as a pathology, or as a continuing hardship inflicted from the era of slavery to the era of mass

incarceration, those who embrace Black family today see the experiments in living together found in Black households, often led by wise women, as models to which all should aspire. A fatherless home is not necessarily a household without a needed role model. It is likely a home with multiple role models, with distinct and overlapping authority: precisely what is needed to navigate the complexities of a world filled with domination. Anchoring Black family, and so anchoring Black dignity, is the figure of the mother: it is she who remains a source of hope when the forces of the world close in. Hence George Floyd's dying words before he was asphyxiated by police: "Momma, I love you. Tell my kids I love them. I'm dead."[3]

From the white, patriarchal perspective, we are made who we are by our inheritance, secured by the legitimacy of our paternity. Which is to say: a man comes into himself by means of his father. A man receives his dignity from his father, and his father from his father's father. Some deserve dignity because of their ancestry, and others do not; we are only a handful of decades removed from the era when nobility was dignity's primary definition. European and North American attempts to democratize dignity, to ascribe it to all human beings, have not purged it of its patriarchal residuum. We have found new fathers: the state, or in some contexts the church, steps in to play the patriarchal role of guarantor of dignity. Whether it is a biological father or a state acting as father, dignity is assured by following another's rules, even as those rules promise and yet foreclose the possibility of self-determination. To inherit from the father, one must not be disowned. The father administers a world of do's and don'ts that supposedly train the son for independence in the world; if the son ignores the father's commands too often, he risks being disowned. Similarly for others who promise dignity: their promises seem unconditional but are actually premised on a level of compliance with the normative order established by the guarantor. There may no longer be an explicit threat of disinheritance, but there are subtler ways of disappearing a person or a people from the spaces where dignity could be recognized. Not everyone gets their day in court.

Blacks in America are "bastards," according to James Baldwin's evocative refrain—in the context of our families, but also in the context of our nation and humanity itself. As Ralph Ellison puts it in *Invisible Man*, "We share a common disinheritance." One response to this realization is to clamor for legitimacy by engaging in respectability politics. Another response is to embrace illegitimacy, to understand it as a gift, an insight that reveals the lie holding up the regime of inheritance. That regime is the site where racial domination and male domination entwine and become one. The master is not just white, he is a white father. Other figures—women, single men, Blacks, people of other races—exist in a world where the white father is preeminent. Embracing illegitimacy challenges this world: it is a challenge that Blacks are in a privileged position to mount, but the challenge benefits all, including the white fathers who, believing the lies about their authority, so misperceive themselves and their world that they become incapable of genuine intimacy.[4]

To embrace disinheritance is to believe that dignity is not a status passed down from a father or lawgiver but an act performed collectively, in the struggle against those who would erase our humanity. Black family names the intimacy of those who share disinheritance and who stand in opposition to the regime of inheritance. In this way, Black family nurtures Black dignity; Black dignity is impossible without Black family. Whereas fashionable terms like Black sociality and Black relationality, as well as earlier terms like Black brotherhood and Black community, attempt to name the affect and activity that constitute shared Black experience, Black family names them in a context where Blackness is defined by twinned racial and gender domination.

The affect and activity of Black family, Black love, and Black rage, conjoined and shaped into struggle, name the intimacy of those who not only suffer together and find joy in each other but who struggle together, whose sufferings and joys and struggles are one and the same.

The inheritance from which Blacks are excluded is not only or even primarily financial and social capital. In a world ruled by patriarchy, white fathers initiate their sons into a normative order. They teach right and wrong on a small scale so that white sons will know how to do right and avoid wrong as full members of society. White children learn from their fathers how to habitually act rightly in the right circumstances, how to be habitually courageous, patient, truthful, generous, and grateful, how to judge rightly. The father plays the role for his family that the king plays for the nation and that God plays for the universe: each is the master of a normative order, and each expects those under him to enter into that order. To be good is to do what God, king, or father says one should do: this is the white, patriarchal social imaginary.

"I've always tried to do the right thing," says Ralph Ellison's Invisible Man, but he inevitably fails. A Black authority, a Black master of a normative order—a Black master—is an oxymoron. The Invisible Man remembers a phrase that has been inside his mind since childhood, "If you're white, you're right." Black fatherhood cannot fulfill the task of fatherhood as defined by the white world. Whatever norms the Black father would set up for his family can be arbitrarily quashed by whites—by an encounter with police, or bureaucrats, or even a teacher. James Baldwin recounts how his sense of his father's omnipotence was shattered when a white teacher, taking an interest in the budding talent of the youth, entered their home to ask permission to bring James to a play. Baldwin's father, who frowned on the theater, was left mute, obsequious. The young Baldwin did not feel relief or a sense of freedom but hatred toward his father, who had been revealed as an imposter. Here begins the gift of disinheritance. Fathers, kings, and gods present themselves as benevolent guarantors of the normative order. In fact they are masters, arbitrarily imposing their wills on their subjects. Rage is the fitting response to domination. But rage requires collectivity to find its proper shape, to sharpen its aim. For Baldwin, this meant shifting from rage at his Black father to rage at the systems of racial and gender domination that negated his Black father as an authority.[5]

Black rage needs its mate, Black love. Those who struggle together, whether the struggles are monumental or mundane, become family. Just as an account of struggle cannot be exhausted by a description of the present but must place present struggle as part of a history stretching back for generations, Black family must include both those who struggle now and their ancestors, those who struggled before. Struggle involves working collectively to name systems of domination and to discern the optimal tactics to attack them. Struggle goes awry if it is an individual enterprise, or if it is only the living who count. The dead must have their vote. Their collective experience and wisdom outweigh any experience I or my generation can accumulate. It is difficult to hear what they have to tell us, but it is also difficult to hear what a family member in the same room has to tell me—and it is difficult to hear what my own experience and wisdom have to tell me. In each case, communication is inevitably clouded, but we work tirelessly to achieve clarity. Such work is part of the struggle.

When Black feminists met as the Combahee River Collective in the late 1970s to articulate their shared political vision, the statement that resulted began by naming ancestors: Sojourner Truth, Frances Harper, Ida Wells, Mary Church Terrell, and Harriet Tubman (who led an attack by a group of Black soldiers in the Civil War that resulted in the liberation of 750 slaves along South Carolina's Combahee River, from which the collective took its name). The Black feminist struggle in the present, the collective wrote, "is the outgrowth of countless generations of personal sacrifice, militancy, and work by our mothers and sisters." Struggle happens collectively among sisters, and it requires the participation of ancestors (mothers). This expansive, porous community of those who struggle is bound together by "a healthy love for ourselves, our sisters, and our community." Black family bound by Black love animates Black struggle and makes possible Black dignity.[6]

The title of Richard Wright's most famous novel, *Native Son*, indicates that it will ask, and not answer, questions of fatherhood. Who could the father be, to make a Black "son" native? The novel is about futile attempts by whites to father Blacks into nativeness, to serve as Black fathers. This is necessary because Black fatherhood has been explicitly destroyed. We are told that the father of Bigger Thomas, the protagonist, was killed during race riots in the South. There was, of course, no justice: "Nothing, far as I know," was done about it, Bigger reports. This narrative of fatherhood is further complicated by the news that Bigger may have white blood. If the novel's title were not enough to point us toward the theme of contested paternity, the central female character, whose death at Bigger's hands propels the narrative forward, is suggestively named Mary. She presents white innocence but also paternity contested: she renounces her father's values and turns to Communism for a new sort of inheritance. Mary has a father—indeed two, one biological and one ideological—and can choose between them, whereas Bigger came of age with his father gone and fatherhood put under erasure by white supremacy.[7]

For Wright, even a Black father who is present cannot fulfill the role, cannot usher a child into the world of norms—because, of course, the white world is foreclosed, and Black life is always illicit. In his memoir, *Black Boy*, Wright describes his father as the "lawgiver" but also distant. "He was always a stranger to me, always somehow alien and remote." Where fatherhood functions properly, in the white world, the child receives a reprimand for a transgression and then learns the norm. When structures of domination make learning the norm impossible, this dynamic is thrown off. "I knew that I would be punished if I did not obey," Wright reports, but he transgresses nonetheless. The book opens with the young Wright literally destroying his father's dominion: he accidentally burns the family's house down. His father's reprimands are similarly out of proportion, with little relationship to a world of norms. "I was lashed so hard and long," he reports, "that I lost consciousness. I was beaten out of my senses." Then his father abandons the family for good, leaving them without a source of income and perpetually short on food, and Wright feels a hunger that is both literal and existential, perhaps theological. (One version of the memoir is titled *American Hunger*.)[8]

The novel *Native Son* is driven by the same existential hunger, the same sense of fatherlessness and meaninglessness, or godlessness, but the outcome, instead of the act of writing, is murder. When whites claim to sate his hunger and serve as his father, Bigger Thomas sees only hollowness. He throws away the cross offered by a white preacher who calls him "son." To a political advertisement positioning a white candidate as an upstanding law-follower, Bigger responds, "You crook." He compares whiteness to a father (and a God) who has cast out his Black children. As Bigger puts it, "They own everything. They choke you off the face of the earth. They like God . . . I'm just a black and they make the laws." That power of whiteness is embodied in Bigger's employer, a real estate tycoon who sees himself as liberal. As the Black servant Peggy is showing Bigger around his new employer's house, she comments, "It's just like one big family." Bigger reflects, "Mr. Dalton was somewhere far away, high up, distant, like a god."

Mr. Dalton's white opponents, revolutionary socialists, function in precisely the same role as Mr. Dalton with respect to Bigger's normative world. While insisting that Bigger not call them "sir," the young revolutionaries do not disrupt the essential relationship of servitude, and by disclaiming that relationship, they bind Bigger even more tightly under their arbitrary will. Wright tells us, "He felt ensnared in a tangle of deep shadows."[9]

White substitute fatherhood fails, but so does Black substitute fatherhood. Imprisoned for Mary's murder, Bigger is visited by a Black preacher who calls him "son" over and over, urging reconciliation with Bigger's heavenly father through himself as the earthly substitute father. But Bigger "loathed" the preacher's words because they "made him feel as condemned and guilty as the voice of those who hated him." Literally imprisoned by whiteness, Bigger sinks lower and lower emotionally, "to the lowest point this side of death"—and then comes back to life. His resurrection is made possible by his resolution to trust no one but himself, to reject all fathers, to reject the need for a father.[10]

This resolution is unsatisfactory. The novel's strength is in the problem it sets out, a problem about divine and human fatherhood. The work of the novel, its beauty, is in dramatizing solutions to this problem that go awry—that result in more domination. James Baldwin reads *Native Son* as a failure. For Baldwin, Wright's title demands legitimacy, acceptance by a father, rather than interrogating the need for a father. Bigger Thomas accepts the authority of the white world, which means that he desires to be inducted into the false religion, the idolatry, of whiteness. His rage at the white world mirrors the white world's rage at him; in accepting himself as a "problem" in white terms he has denied his own Black humanity. Wright compounds Bigger's ailment by depicting him in social isolation, removed from family and community, and from himself. For Baldwin, this simply reproduces the white denial of Black humanity. It ignores the complexity of Black life in the context of white supremacy, a complexity that is the key to struggling against racial domination. Baldwin worries that Wright understands only the negative component of Black family, the critique of patriarchy, and that only poorly; Wright misses the positive component, the intense affection joining those who struggle together.[11]

Baldwin's own writing is more continuous with Wright's than he let on. Unsurprisingly: Wright ushered Baldwin into the New York literary world. The younger writer found in Wright "my ally and my witness, and alas! my father." The sorrowful interjection marks Baldwin's failure to find a father, a failure with the same cause as all such failures. The prospective father seems authoritative, seems to offer security and a home. He offers to create a "native son," but for Black Americans, that is an oxymoron. Baldwin's view of fatherhood was precisely the opposite of Barack Obama's and Bill Cosby's. Whereas they saw Black fathers as necessary, stabilizing forces, pillars of the Black community, Baldwin's life's work, like Wright's, was to transform Black fatherhood from an answer into a question. By attacking the twinned racist, patriarchal logics that place Black fathers at the head of Black families, Baldwin opens up space for valuing Black intimacy and for embracing a porous but not amorphous sense of Black family.[12]

Baldwin was haunted by the question: Whose little boy are you? He was asked this by his first minister, in the church where he was to open his heart to God. It was a question he had heard frequently on the streets of Harlem, posed by pimps and hoodlums. And it was the question he felt Elijah Muhammad was posing to him when the Nation of Islam leader welcomed Baldwin, by then an acclaimed writer, into his Chicago home. It was a question about authority and allegiance—with the interrogative mood underscoring the fluidity of both. "Notes of a

Native Son," the grand autobiographical essay that is the centerpiece of Baldwin's first essay collection, responds to the question *whose little boy are you?* by attempting to do what Wright did not: fill out the complexities of Black social life and inner life. The claim to be a native is unmistakably ironic. Baldwin does not demand that his filial legitimacy be recognized but instead displays the inescapable complications of filiation. He does not demand that his humanity be recognized; he performs his humanity. He ponders, reasons, emotes; he writes. What he writes is a story of his father that is also a story of his own coming of age, and a story of racial injustice in America. These all coincide in the opening lines of the essay, where Baldwin declares that, over two days, his father (a minister) died, his mother gave birth to a child, he himself turned nineteen, and race riots broke out in New York City.

Authority collapses: a father dies. Baldwin's father, a preacher, is an almost mythical figure. No one is certain of his age. He was handsome and proud and very dark. He reminds Baldwin of "African tribal chieftains," wearing war paint, holding a spear. His power, it would seem, came from time immemorial and was sanctioned by the heavens; indeed, it comes from the heavens. Baldwin describes his father as living in "unimaginably close communion with the Lord," often staring into space, his silence "punctuated by moans and hallelujahs." This frightening, otherworldly father imposed his will on his children with physical force. His decisions, and his blows, could not be appealed. And his apparent intimacy with the Lord gave his words divine sanction; it made visceral God's reign. For those he ruled, his family, this Black father was God.[13]

Yet this god-father's absolute authority was undermined by the white world. Baldwin's father raged out of control, eventually went mad. It was a madness centered on the impossibility of his position, the impossibility of his authority. And it was a madness that eventually caused his death. The dead father did not need to respond in this way to Black life, though it is a very natural way to respond. There is also the possibility of renewed life, represented by the birth of Baldwin's brother on the day his father died. The young James Baldwin came of age at this moment by realizing that he could not, must not, choose his father's madness and must instead choose new life—choose Black family.

What remains, according to Baldwin, after the overbearing father is made precarious, after his authority is undermined by the world, is love. This is how we can all truly become brothers, how we can become family. The love we receive from our fathers may feel disordered or stifling; Baldwin's father's love was "outrageously demanding and protective." We must remember, though, that love is love, even if its manifestations are distorted by worldly forces. The question "Whose little boy are you?" is also a question of love. It asks whether love can be prostituted, whether it can be offered without commitment. The domineering father of Baldwin's debut novel, *Go Tell It on the Mountain*, as well as the domineering God-the-Father whom the novel's protagonist, John Grimes, comes to embrace, form the backbone of the narrative. But at the novel's heart is John's sometimes playful but decidedly sensual embrace of Elisha, an older boy whose appearance is the only unequivocal beauty—and perhaps goodness and truth—to be found in the book. The novel ends with Elisha offering the protagonist a "holy kiss" and assuring him, "God won't forget you." Once God is no longer identified with father, intimacy and sensuality can expand the bounds of family. But because Baldwin never fully couples love and struggle, his work may be read as advocating watery, undirected love, love that does not move in the shape of justice—and thus enters the multiculturalist canon.[14]

Black feminist intellectuals have shared Wright's and Baldwin's suspicion of deified fathers, but they have also provided richer accounts of the complex social life and alternative modes of authority that result when patriarchy is resisted. Consider Alice Walker's *The Color Purple*, consisting of letters written by the protagonist, Celie. At first she writes to God; later, as God recedes along with the patriarchal authority he represents, she writes to another woman. Celie's letters began as part of a search for an alternative father because her stepfather was abusing her. She even capitalizes *He* when referring to her stepfather as if referring to God. Her stepfather does not create a stable normative universe, so she turns to a higher authority, a God who never writes back. Celie's abusive stepfather tells her that she is evil, a liar, promiscuous— all these accusations she confesses to her God. But as God recedes, fathers recede: a letter midway through the text reveals, "Pa is not our Pa!" He had always been an impersonal, distant authority who presented himself as her real father. "I never even remember Ma calling him by his name. She always said, Your Pa." It turns out that her father was lynched, that he has no grave—he continues to haunt. Where Bigger Thomas and Ellison's Invisible Man turned to male father substitutes, Celie turns to a woman, Shug, who by definition cannot function as a father substitute and who therefore complicates the role of father. Shug, as her lover, commands familial allegiance: "Us each other's people now." The role of father (and God) is unnecessary in this world of women loving women. It is against this context, from this community of women, that the critique of father-idols becomes possible—in contrast to the solitary struggles against father-idols dramatized by Wright and Ellison. Celie realizes, "The God I been praying and writing to is a man. And just like all the other mens I know. Trifling, forgetful and lowdown. . . . He big and old and tall and gray-bearded and white. He wear white robes and go barefooted."[15]

Walker, like Wright, frames the question of paternity in spiritual terms. Shug embraces her life as a "sinner," not worried about divine or paternal reprimand. What matters in her theology is pure, unadulterated love. If God is loving, she preaches to Celie, there are no obliga-tions, just warm embrace. There is no need to follow moral codes or institutional religions unless a person desires it. "Any God I ever felt in church I brought in with me. And I think all the other folks did too. They come to church to *share* God, not find God." Shug goes on to ex-pound a whole system of religious-humanist beliefs. God is inside every-one. God has no gender. God loves all feelings and allows you to enjoy your own feelings. God's one imperative is to appreciate self and world, to take notice of the color purple in a field. In short, we can be our own gods; we can, ourselves, fulfill the role of father. Like Wright, Walker writes beautifully when she poses a question, but turns pedantic as she offers her answer—even as that answer is ostensibly describing beauty.[16]

Audre Lorde is a more rigorous thinker and writer than Walker on the question of fatherhood. She poses the problem of authority and ostensibly rejects father figures, yet she does not purge them en-tirely from her writing. Like Wright, Baldwin, and Walker, Lorde offers a story of self-assertion told through self-assertion: spinning her own myth, what she labels her "biomythography." But she does this with a playfulness that allows her to toy with, rather than outright reject, the question of authority.[17]

On the surface, Lorde's narrative is a story without fathers. In *Zami*'s opening lines we read, "My father leaves his psychic print upon me, silent, intense, and unforgiving. But his is a distant light-ning. Images of women flaming like torches adorn and define the borders of my journey, stand like dykes between me and the chaos." A community of Black women will make life possible, will provide the conditions of possibility for worldly engagement and struggle, for cri-tique. In *Zami*, a father is present and absent at once, an acknowledg-ment of norms, of authority, but not the heart of the world. Unlike Walker, Lorde from the start portrays the world of women into which she will guide the reader as morally ambivalent. Her journey, she writes, consists of "images of women, kind and cruel." Like Walker, she treats sensuality as sacred. She writes, "The sound of our bodies meeting is the prayer of all strangers and sisters, that the discarded evils, abandoned at all crossroads, will not follow us upon our journeys." Note that this sacred sensuality is not an antinomian land in which to wallow. It is a practice that entails discarding evils and continuing forward—where one will certainly encounter more evils.[18]

Lorde opens *Zami* with the question of authority posed when fathers are set aside. She asks, "To whom do I owe the power behind my voice?" Her ideal, and an implicit answer to her query, is not a godlike man but a neighbor woman, DeLois. This woman was poor, had "bad" hair and a "big proud stomach." She was not in the least like God, but she elicited fear and desire at a primordial level. Lorde writes, "I loved her because she moved like she felt she was somebody special, like she was somebody I'd like to know someday. She moved like how I thought god's mother must have moved, and my mother, once upon a time, and someday maybe me." DeLois is Blackness unadulterated, undominated. She "seemed to laugh all over."[19]

Among her sources of power, along with DeLois, Lorde recalls her own ancestors. Her story of her mother's mother's mothers, in Grenada, is about communities of women loving each other, strong and beautiful—but also absent, distant historically and geographically as well as conceptually. The sense of the tragic, of the ever broken, ever distanced nature of the world, and the ever opaque nature of authority is brought home to Lorde because of her Blackness. When she takes a white woman as a lover, she finds sensual spirituality, but it is always suffused with brokenness. She writes, "Muriel seemed to believe that as lesbians, we were all outsiders and all equal in our outsiderhood. 'We're all niggers,' she used to say, and I hated to hear her say it. It was wishful thinking based on little fact." Blackness and anti-Blackness, as systems of domination, are constitutive of Lorde's world.

They are not even momentarily overcome by love. To believe they could be is a fantasy born of domination itself. Lorde writes, "Each one of us had been starved for love for so long that we wanted to believe that love, once found, was all-powerful. We wanted to believe that it could give word to my inchoate pain and rages; that it could enable Muriel to face the world and get a job; that it could free our writings, cure racism, end homophobia and adolescent acne."[20]

Yet even in a world of domination, impossibly broken, Lorde found in her mother a model of authority without a father's authoritarianism. She found sensuality, but not as an unequivocal source of authority; she found attachment, but always with difficulty. She found a woman struggling against domination but not living undominated: her mother was still Black and female in a white patriarchal world. Lorde's mother was treated as an authority by others in the community: they would instinctively defer to her, whether in the meat market, on the bus, or asking directions on the street. Her mother would not take charity. She constructed a normative universe for her daughter even in the face of white domination. Lorde recalls, "As a child, the most horrible condition I could contemplate was being wrong and being discovered. Mistakes could mean exposure, maybe even annihilation. In my mother's house, there was no room in which to make errors, no room to be wrong."[21]

On one hand, Lorde's mother seemed above emotion. When the young Audre lost a student council election due to racism, her mother responded briskly, "Wipe your face. Start acting like a human being!" On the other hand, Lorde writes movingly of "the rhythms of a litany, the rituals of Black women combing their daughters' hair," another spiritual-sensual experience that would hint at pure presence, perfect communion—but then she complicates the narrative. Her mother's hands are "strong" and "rough," her own shoulders are "rebellious," "hunched and jerking." This liturgy is difficult, painful; for Lorde's mother, "the sensual content of life was masked and cryptic." Her mother's authority, despite being "divine," was imperfect. It was not domineering like the authority Lorde encountered among her friends' fathers, but it was overbearing. As Lorde puts it, "My mother viewed any act of separation from her as an indictment of her authority." Audre's bedroom door always had to be open; her mother was always in her business. Surely these flaws responded to racial and gender domination; our world is full of domination. Authorities will always be flawed, and that is what Lorde calls on us to recognize. Unlike Walker, she does not place ultimate authority in her own hands. She invokes the authority of her sisters and mothers, her Black family.[22]

While *The Color Purple* was wildly popular, Walker's challenge to patriarchy was interpreted as an attack on Black men, causing great controversy. Her mainstream reception today is primarily as a love mystic—an explainer of Black women's culture who adds to the multicultural rainbow. Lorde's *Zami*, with its rigorous interrogation of Black family relationships and its insistent orientation toward struggle at every level, was a hit among radical feminists who embraced Lorde's attack on patriarchy, but unlike *The Color Purple* it was never a *New York Times* best seller. During the era of multiculturalism, Black women's experiences may have been valued, but patriarchy, like white supremacy, remained intact.

This is crystal clear in the 1995 memoir of that crowning figure of the era, Barack Obama. Like Wright, Ellison, and Baldwin before him, Obama begins his "story of race and inheritance" without a father. The book opens with Obama receiving a phone call informing him that the father he has barely known is dead. The memoir is structured around a search for substitute fathers, for alternative sources of authority: he tries out his stepfather; his grandfather; Black nationalist college students; poor women whom he would organize on Chicago's

South Side; Harold Washington, the first Black mayor of Chicago; and the Christian God. None is up to the challenge. Obama's longing for a father figure is sated only when he travels to Africa and receives from relatives a full account of his biological father's life story.[23]

Ta-Nehisi Coates functions as a bridge figure between the era of multiculturalism and our current moment. Coates attracted a huge amount of popular attention for explaining (largely to white liberals) just how deeply anti-Black racism is felt on the lives and bodies of Black Americans. In line with movement activists, he diagnosed racial domination as a problem that policy fixes would not solve, however laudable and necessary they might be. Note the form his lament took: *Between the World and Me* is structured as a letter to Coates's son, complete with father-son photos. Coates's previous book, his memoir *A Beautiful Struggle*, is organized around maturing into his relationship with his father. For Coates, like Obama, Black struggle takes a patriarchal form: both writers struggle to be good sons, then to be good fathers. They believe Black dignity can be achieved through respectability, through fulfilling a role that is in fact structurally impossible for Black Americans to fulfill. While Wright, Ellison, and Baldwin name Black fatherhood as a problem that can never be solved, Obama and Coates proffer solutions. Once Obama comes to know his father, he can confidently chart a path to the presidency, to become a father to the nation. Once Coates comes to terms with his father, he can embrace their shared African heritage, beat on the *djembe* he holds between his legs—become a man.[24]

A generation of Black activists and writers who are younger than Coates and Obama recall growing up with absent fathers, yet that absence does not structure their lives or narratives. They find comfort and provisional authority in Black women, friends, and ancestors: in Black family. These writers are more often poor than middle class, but they do not aspire to the mores that would make them respectable.

They take intersectionality seriously, explicitly naming and analyzing how racial and gender domination has poisoned their lives. Darnell Moore recounts the abuse he and his mother suffered from his father. After years of absence, Moore runs into his father late one night on his way home from an evening in the Philadelphia gay scene. Moore is blinded by rage at his father, but then he realizes that this is the same rage that fuels his activism, his struggle against racial domination. He no longer needs to be enraged at his father; his rage has been shaped and directed at more fitting targets.[25]

Patrisse Cullors's mother grew up a Jehovah's Witness, got pregnant, and was shunned by her community. While Cullors's memoir ends with the author becoming a mother herself, it is not structured around a journey to motherhood or coming to terms with her mother. Rather, Cullors tells a story of building her own family, gathering friends and loved ones around her, navigating the tensions of intimacy while struggling together. Her mother is no substitute father. In fact, when Cullors's mentally ill brother is caught up in the criminal justice system, Cullors is enraged at his ill treatment, but her mother can only weep, explaining to her daughter that she weeps out of guilt. This puzzles Cullors until she realizes that for her mother, overwhelmed by patriarchal and racial domination, the expected maternal emotions were blocked. Her mother never felt righteous indignation, nor did she feel pride or joy, hope or wholeness. Her whole being was oriented to her children's survival: to protecting them, grieving when they suffered harm, feeling guilt that her protection was inadequate. Like Baldwin, Cullors invites us to reflect not on how to become our parents but on how domination has unmade our parents, motivating us to live differently. Cullors herself is able to experience the full range of emotions as a mother because unlike her mother, she has gathered around her a community with which she can struggle: Black family.[26]

5

Black Futures

The civil rights movement was fueled by hope. Its anthem, "We Shall Overcome," and its most famous oration, "I Have a Dream," put hope front and center. Engraved on the Martin Luther King, Jr., memorial in Washington, DC, are the words "Out of a mountain of despair, a stone of hope." These words inspired the design of the monument itself, with King's figure emerging out of an uncarved "mountain." Given the entrenchment of racial domination and the long odds that protest would be successful, those organizing for Black freedom could only have been motivated by hope—or so conventional wisdom holds.

Today, hope hardly figures in the moral vocabulary of the Black Lives Matter movement. In part this has to do with a turn away from Christianity, tainted by its association with respectability; hope is a very Christian sentiment. Hope also becomes suspect because of the depths of anti-Blackness and the sense, which has become central to activists' analysis, that racial domination is invincible. Those who hoped in the past have been disappointed. The civil rights movement's hopes for an end to segregation resulted in de jure segregation becoming de facto segregation, and in the rise of an even more vicious regime for managing Black bodies and souls: mass incarceration. Hope seems futile.

Except for one hope. Black activists and theorists today often talk about "the end of the world." The only possibility of flourishing will be after the end of the world. Racism and other forms of domination so contaminate the world that only after it ends will we be free. One point of origin for this view is *Notebook of a Return to a Native Land* by the Black Caribbean writer Aimé Césaire, a poetic masterpiece first written in 1939 and rewritten over the next two decades. Césaire left his home in the French colony of Martinique to study at the preeminent French college, the École normale supérieure, the alma mater of Jean-Paul Sartre, Simone Weil, Michel Foucault, and Jacques Derrida. There he founded and edited *The Black Student*, a literary magazine whose contributors would become leading lights of the Francophone Black intellectual world. Césaire's *Notebook* reflects on what it means to see his home island and its people from the perspective of one who has traveled abroad, connected with other Blacks from around the world, and must now negotiate his relationship to his home. "What can I do?" Césaire ponders.

> One must begin somewhere.
> Begin what?
> The only thing in the world worth beginning:
> The End of the world of course.

He believes his task is not to improve or reform Martinican society, or French society. The rage that he and his fellow students feel must be shaped in a way that precipitates society's collapse—and that encourages imagining life after domination.[1]

Black studies scholar Frank Wilderson, whose theoretical idiom has migrated into activist spaces, has made Césaire's call for "the End of the world" integral to his own vision of "Afropessimism." "Antiblack violence is a paradigm of oppression for which there is no coherent form of redress," Wilderson writes. The only thing to be done: hope for the end of the world and struggle to achieve it. He describes how, at a political meeting he attended that was meant to gather a spectrum of people of color for coalition-building, the specificity of anti-Blackness was erased. But when the meeting split into breakout rooms organized by race—Blacks, Latinos, Asians, Native Americans, whites—the conversation rapidly changed. Instead of a "politics of culture," those in the Black breakout room talked about a "culture of politics." No longer was Black suffering forced into analogy with other forms of suffering. Instead, the Black participants (mainly non-academics) seamlessly moved from talk of microaggressions to police violence to slavery, clearly understanding that the same structure of domination animated all three. In an all-Black space, the orientation toward struggle and collective analysis of domination came naturally and effervescently: "Folks cried and laughed and hugged each other and called out loud for the end of the world. No one poured cold water on this by asking, What does that mean—the end of the world?" It was obvious that domination must end, requiring the world to end. Not only was there shared analysis and commitment to struggle, "the dangerous fuse of the Black imagination had been lit by nothing more than the magic of an intramural conversation."[2]

How to Survive the End of the World is a podcast launched in 2017 by Black activists and sisters Adrienne Marie and Autumn Brown. Evoking anxieties about climate change as well as anti-Blackness, the Brown sisters interview community organizers, writers, and move-ment leaders who are experimenting with new ways of living together on a deteriorating planet. Their conversations give some attention to naming and analyzing systems of domination, but even more impor-tant is the Black imagination, envisioning possible futures. They found the work of Black science fiction writer Octavia Butler particu-larly inspirational. Butler's fiction from the 1990s speculated about how global collapse, brought about by climate change and unfettered capitalism, might permit communities of marginalized people to build new societies from the ground up in the shadow of the violently disintegrating old world. "Science fiction is simply a way to practice the future together," Adrienne Marie Brown writes. "It is our right and responsibility to create a new world."[3]

Instead of hope, those who struggle for Black justice today talk about Black futures, a label that joins a sense of the anti-Black world's demise and the imperative to imagine radically new ways of living together. In 2016, two years after its founding, the network of grass-roots groups organizing under the label of Black Lives Matter began designating February (traditionally celebrated as Black History Month) Black Futures Month. While there would still be a role for remembering Black ancestors, "Black Futures Month challenges us to envision and construct a world where Black people are liberated," a "future for Black folks centered in Black joy, love, restoration, and healing." Activist Alicia Garza created a spin-off nonprofit, the Black Futures Lab, dedicated to helping Black communities imagine collectively—and then, based on that vision, examine what policy changes could move the world toward that future. While this approach seems incompatible with Césaire's, as reformism is at odds with a revolutionary spirit, in both cases the emphasis on imagining futures, rather than hoping, underscores the need to pivot to a new genre. Whether it is through an embrace of science fiction, poetry, or exclamation, prosaic planning and strategizing are subordinated to collective imagination.[4]

Black futures describe a free world, a world without domination and therefore qualitatively different from our own. There is a chasm between here and there that systematic thought, scientific calculation, and precise planning will never bridge. We cannot get there, and we cannot know what it is like over there. Every description is contaminated by the present, by the interlocking systems of domination that fill our world and not only impose their will on us bodily and scar our souls, but also infect our desires. They set the terms of what can be done and what can be thought and felt—and hoped.

Some theorists distinguish optimism, the belief that unlikely but desired outcomes will occur, from hope, the belief that some yet-unimagined outcome will turn out to be even better than what we desired. Whereas optimism fixes on specific objects, hope peers beyond the horizon of possibility. The more we fix on specific, visible objects, the less open we are to being surprised by what we cannot see; the more optimistic we are, the less hopeful. Unfortunately, in ordinary language, hope and optimism are often conflated. The 2008 Republican vice presidential candidate Sarah Palin put her finger on this when she dismissed hope, Barack Obama's slogan, as "that hopey changey stuff." Obama was disguising familiar liberal public policy goals behind the grand rhetoric of hope. He could get away with it because his rhetorical performance mimicked that of the Black public preacher made famous by Martin Luther King, Jr. King's theological vision of hope aimed beyond the world became, in Obama's hands, secularized into an ambition for making the world slightly better— really overstuffed optimism. Obama is not the only culprit. The rhetoric of hope, and Christian theological reflection on hope, has long equivocated between hope and optimism, resulting in hope tainted by worldly interests and optimism inflated by otherworldly imaginings.[5]

Recent activists have been more clear about the divide between the present and their desired futures, marking this chasm with the phrase "the end of the world." The only way to describe those futures is in the tainted language of the present; to successfully conjure futures, language must be expanded, turned in on itself, or scrambled. We must resist the temptation to hear this talk of futures literally. When King unforgettably speaks of "the day when all of God's children, Black and white men, Jews and Gentiles, Protestants and Catholics, will be able to join hands and sing in the words of the old Negro spiritual 'Free at last,' " it is easy to forget that he is speaking of a *dream*. To evoke a world where domination is no more, King speaks in a register where language and images are always jumbled, and then appeals to a song. Dreams, music, poetry, art, mysticism, and science fiction can motivate us without dictating a particular course of action. They remind us that the present world does not have the last word, that the world can be free, and that we love freedom. Put another way, conjuring Black futures motivates but does not dictate the struggle against domination, breathing life into Black dignity. No future, no dignity.

Black futures and Black pasts are asymmetrical. Looking forward, we must distinguish two registers: the register of the visible future in which we predict, calculate, and strategize, and the register of the invisible, eschatological Black future, qualitatively different from the present. When we look backward, time falls into only one register. Certainly domination in the present contaminates both our forward-looking and backward-looking perspectives, but this happens in different ways. Domination cuts off access to futures after the end of the world, leaving us to desire only the possibilities offered by domination itself. The slave is told she has no escape, she must live and feel and dream in the master's world. In the other direction, domination shapes the past we receive, foregrounding some stories and pushing others to the background. Slaves are taught that Africans have no history, that history is European. Domination also shapes our affective relationship to the past, making us melancholic, or nostalgic for the triumphs of earlier generations (what Nietzsche calls monumentalism), or ostensibly clear-eyed but actually obsessed with confirming every detail of the stories we have been told (what Nietzsche calls antiquarianism). Monumentalism and antiquarianism both naturalize domination, confirming through facts and feelings the story domination tells about itself to conceal its brutal force. In fact, history begins in the primal scene of domination: slavery; it ends with the end of the world, when all domination is eliminated. History begins with slavery because it is through the filter of slavery and its afterlives, through the filter of domination, that all history is told. That primal scene exists outside of history as its condition of possibility. By conjuring Black futures, we make visible the reality of domination, and we begin to see how it warps history.[6]

But what of counter-histories, histories from below, histories of struggle against domination? These are best told in prose. They are best understood as tactical interventions in a domain controlled by the forces of domination. They are a means of gathering arms for the present struggle, motivated by the needs of the present struggle. If such histories aspire to more, if they aim to provide grand narratives of the oppressed, their readers forget that these histories, too, are contaminated by domination. The monumental and antiquarian temptations affect historians of the oppressed as much as they affect historians comfortably aligned with the status quo. These tendencies are countered not only by intellectual rigor but also by communities of accountability. Do the stories told about ancestors in struggle resonate with those immersed in struggle today? Similarly for futurists: do the stories told, now in a different genre, about life after the end of the world resonate with communities immersed in struggle today? If not, they are most likely contaminated by worldly interests, tainted with the stench of domination.

In 1986, thanks to a bill signed by Ronald Reagan, the United States began celebrating Martin Luther King, Jr., Day as a national holiday. Reagan lauded King for giving "eloquent voice and powerful leadership to the long-cherished hopes of millions." That year, a 736-page collection of King's writings was published under the title *A Testament of Hope*, reflecting the widespread understanding of him as icon of hope. In it we find King's thoughts on nonviolence, civil disobedience, love, racial integration, and movement strategy. Curiously, hope itself is addressed so fleetingly that it is absent from the volume's index. This reflects a broader fact about how we remember King: hope is dramatically over-ascribed to him. Indeed, at the monument in Washington, King *is* hope. He is representative of the way hope figures in the American imagination: white Americans *have* hope, Black Americans *are* hope, bodily. Just as Black Americans are thought to be especially emotional and especially spiritual, we are thought to be especially hopeful.[7]

The condescending white gaze further presumes that, given our pitiful condition, Blacks must spend much of our time hoping. This emotional logic accompanies the superordinate perspective on alterity in general: you are not like us, so you must hope to be like us—"must" being both descriptive and normative. In some contexts of domination, the object of hope, from the perspective of those who dominate, is cure. Something ails a person or a community; once that ailment is removed, once it is cured, the one who suffers from it will be free, just like everyone else. Unspoken is the will to destruction implicit in this framing: when the supposed ailment is integral to the being of the person or community who "suffers" from it, cure means destruction of those it purports to save.[8]

Consider the view of homosexuality that was once pervasive. It was seen as a pathology of desire that caused personal and social difficulties, and such desire should be eliminated or redirected. Homosexuality should be "cured." The hope for cure was internalized to some degree by many queer folks themselves, who understood themselves to be captured by pathological desire. After political and social struggle clarified the extent to which queer folks are subject to domination, the desire for cure went away—first among queer folks, then among many in the culture at large. Instead, those institutions and practices that secure and naturalize homophobic domination, such as marriage, employment discrimination, and harassment, became targets of agitation. The struggle against domination was no longer the struggle to cure a pathological condition; now it was a struggle to transform a whole battery of institutions, laws, norms, and words.

Even more dramatically, the emotional lives of people with disabilities is often reduced almost entirely, in the popular imagination, to hope for a cure. Disability rights activists have pointed out that people with disabilities live emotionally complex lives and often report the same quality of life as those without disabilities. Their struggle ought not to be waged exclusively or even primarily in the realm of medicine; the domination of people with disabilities actually happens in the myriad ways ableism is baked into our physical and social worlds.

In both the case of homosexuality and the case of people with disabilities, there is often still a sense that striving for a cure is only misdirected, and that it can be redirected toward more appropriate objects. Framed in this way, worldly optimism still animates the struggle that these marginalized individuals and communities must wage. But when our focus shifts from curing a problem to curing domination, and when we appreciate that domination manifests in interlocking systems, with the domination of queer folks interlocking with the domination of people with disabilities interlocking with patriarchal, racial, and capitalist domination, there is no reason for those who live under domination to hope for anything except the end of the world. For those of us who live in such a context, illusions and false hopes are constant temptations. The struggle against domination includes the struggle to purge false hopes, to orient our hope solely toward the end of the world, and to imagine futures of flourishing after the end of the world. Ascribing hope too freely strengthens the forces of domination, confusing or even erasing the struggles of communities living under domination.

Martin Luther King, Jr., did not talk about hope very much, but when he did, he approached it with intellectual rigor. Indeed, his account of hope resources and prefigures more recent activist talk of Black futures, even as his image as towering prophet is at odds with the bottom-up organizing culture of today's racial justice movement. In the last year of King's life, he delivered a sermon titled "The Meaning of Hope" in Alabama, Detroit, and Los Angeles. As the tumultuous 1960s dragged on, King worried that the national maladies of economic inequality, poverty, materialism, and of course racism were leading toward "spiritual doom." But he cautioned that we must not be tempted to resignation. "Because there is something wrong our struggle must continue," he said. In such a context, hope understood correctly can fuel struggle.[9]

King acknowledged how loosely the word *hope* is used. We must train ourselves, he said, to recognize false copies of hope. One way hope talk goes wrong is for hope to be confused with optimism, "magic hope" that "tomorrow everything will automatically be better." Such a view does not acknowledge the tragic, fallen nature of the world; we, using secular terms, might say that it does not acknowledge the pervasiveness of domination. Another way hope talk goes wrong, according to King, is for hope to affix to objects entirely disconnected from the world. King worried about religious leaders promising bounties in heaven while remaining quiet on how hope could motivate action in the present. We need to appreciate that our objects of hope are impossibly distant from us, yet we can have a foretaste of them. "What is hoped for is in some sense already present," King tells his audiences. But the hoped-for object is always clouded. It cannot be accessed with systematic thought or expressed in prose.[10]

Hope itself, according to King, is found where it is discerned collectively: "hope has a 'we' quality." The more hope we find in those around us, the more hope we ourselves develop. Collectivity does not just increase the quantity of hope, it also increases its quality, refining its object and revealing its counterfeits. King proposes a test: "You can never hope for something that you don't hope for somebody else and for many other selves." If hope cannot be shared, it is mere desire, what one individual covets. What do we hope for everyone to have? Freedom. A world where all are free from domination in every form. We are offered foretastes of freedom in our world, and in the small victories of our struggles, but freedom itself remains a world away— after the end of the world. Hope is essential for life, at least life with dignity, human life as opposed to bare existence. Without a collective dream of freedom, life becomes a mere repetition of what has been done before, what has been said before, what has been thought before. The forces of domination prohibit surprise; mastery thrives in a closed system. When we encounter experiences that challenge that sense of closure, we are primed to struggle against the systems of domination that enforce closure. Those opaque, irreducible experiences in the present—of art, song, poetry, or dreams—offer a foretaste of futures with no domination, after the end of the world.

King tells us we can achieve clarity about hope by reflecting on the experience of "our slave foreparents." He recounts the horrors of the Middle Passage and holds up the persistent hope of those enslaved. They tirelessly pursued freedom, motivated by hope for a world in which no one is enslaved. As a Christian minister, King sees the church as the place where the clarity about hope achieved at the primal scene of slavery (and at the crucifixion) is kept alive and continually clarified in community. As it is preserved, hope does not become an abstract idea or a mere feeling. For King, it flows seamlessly into action, into committed struggle. "Hope is a refusal to give up," he says. In his Christian idiom, he explains hope as Jesus telling us, when we face seemingly insurmountable odds, "Fight on." Yet far from blinding us to the realities we face (the hold domination has over our world), King's hope offers clarity. When we allow the forces of domination to have the last word, we do not see the world rightly. Without hope, ugliness appears beautiful, truth appears false, and goodness appears evil. What seems real is an illusion put forward to make domination seem necessary, "a moral astigmatism." To see and act rightly, to realize our humanity, we must believe we will be free and struggle to achieve our freedom.

There could hardly be two Black intellectuals more different from each other than Martin Luther King, Jr., and Samuel R. Delany. King was a Southern preacher, movement organizer, and trained theologian who became an international media star. Delany is a college dropout and science fiction writer who achieved stardom only in that niche literary world. King spoke extensively about race; Delany writes about it only occasionally, and then makes it subordinate to other concerns. Along with Octavia Butler, Delany is one of the relatively obscure Black intellectuals to whom a younger generation of Black activists look for resources. King is increasingly considered suspect, his charisma entangled with patriarchy, his style of leadership erasing the hard, thankless work of countless grassroots organizers, and his Christianity seen as evincing a desire for respectability. Outside the spotlight, queer, and deeply identified with the working class, Delany offers insights that promise to correct the blind spots of figures like King.[11]

Delany has nothing to say about hope, but he is deeply concerned with imagining futures, and using those futures to motivate struggle against present domination. Much of his imaginative work happens in his fiction, where he creates and probes worlds where domination and struggle take on new forms. But he also published three memoirs, in 1978, 1988, and 1999, each interrogating his own participation in utopian projects. In these books, he aims to demystify utopian experiments, underscoring the difference between a truly free world of the future and experiments in freedom in the present. In the third memoir, he uses his depiction of a utopian experiment to offer an account of domination that addresses contemporary political struggles. In each book he models rigorous, critical history, neither monumental nor antiquarian.

Delany was born in New York in 1942, the grandson of a slave. A gifted student, he attended the Bronx High School of Science (where he was a classmate of Stokely Carmichael) and began to write novels as a teenager. In high school he found intellectual comradery in a Jewish classmate, Marilyn Hacker, and at age nineteen, with Hacker pregnant, the couple took a bus to Detroit to marry. Michigan was the nearest state where a couple their age, of different races, was legally allowed to wed. Through the 1960s, Delany led a bohemian life as an aspiring writer and musician. For a few months during the winter of 1967–68, he lived communally with members of his band, Heavenly Breakfast, as well as their friends and friends of their friends. That winter forms the subject of Delany's 1978 memoir, *Heavenly Breakfast: An Essay on the Winter of Love*, a book explicitly framed as an effort to complicate the too-easy narratives then developing about the 1967 "Summer of Love," colored either by nostalgia for a supposed glimpse of freedom on earth or contempt for the breakdown of social order. Delany contrasts 1967 with the violence that followed—the assassinations of King and Robert Kennedy, the attempt on Andy Warhol's life—but with sympathy for its youthful strivings (the average age in the commune was twenty-two).[12]

Delany and his peers wanted freedom. When we say *freedom*, we are tempted to fill in a picture: what it looks like, how it feels, what procedures are necessary to achieve it. For Delany, the freedom his commune offered was negative: freedom from domination. Such freedom does not look like peace and tranquility, nor does it look like democracy, nor even like consensus-based decision-making. People were bumping into each other, literally and metaphorically, all the time. They were having problems that could only be solved collectively. But outside the world of domination, mutual aid and healing unintended harms flow naturally. When one resident had gonorrhea, other members of the commune quickly noticed (there was no bathroom door) and responded without fuss by bringing him to the hospital. When someone noticed shoes were soiling the floor, he suggested that everyone take their shoes off when entering the apartment, instituting a social practice rather than a rule. "The goad to do something someone wanted you to do was having to live with that person's discomfort or disapproval if you didn't do it. As close as we lived, that was quite a goad." When domination is eliminated, we perceive rightly and act rightly. When we perceive our action causing discomfort to another, we stop.[13]

All those who lived in the commune retained their own shifting sets of preferences and desires. Living together without domination meant allowing oneself to show one's desires and responding to the desires of others, all without hang-ups. Delany distilled this principle, implicit in the commune's practice, into a simple guideline: when you encounter someone's desire, "If it pleases you, you move toward it; if not, you sidestep politely as your individual temperament allows." Put another way, desire was never collectivized, it was negotiated; because of the freedom from domination, those negotiations were effectively effortless, correct perception leading without distortion to fitting response. Achieving this space without domination required balancing between extremes. Delaney describes visiting one commune where everything was shared and there was constant bickering, another where each resident had his or her own room and there was no sense of intimacy. In this world, to find a foretaste of a future without domination, balance is necessary.[14]

In Delany's second and third memoirs, *The Motion of Light in Water* and *Times Square Red, Times Square Blue*, his focus shifts from a physical space, a communal apartment where freedom was practiced, to sites of encounter—first gay bathhouses, then erotic movie theaters. Delany had been inclined toward gay sex and had experienced it, but Greenwich Village's bathhouses were where he could become a gay man. There he witnessed "an undulating mass of naked, male bodies, spread wall to wall," men who had felt deviant but were now confident in who they were. Massed desire obscures difference and domination: "Whether male, female, working or middle class, the first direct sense of political power comes from the apprehension of massed bodies." The feminist historian Joan Scott, writing in 1991 at the height of multiculturalism's power, worried that Delany was embracing a form of identity politics that ceded ultimate authority to personal experience. Through his experiences in the bathhouses, Delany came to know the truth: he was a gay man and millions of gay men exist, even if society and history try to erase them. Scott asked, doesn't Delany flatten multifaceted, ever-shifting human beings into single-identity labels, and doesn't he, by doing so, improperly shift our focus from structures of domination to individual agency? Scott's challenge may be overblown: in *The Motion of Light in Water* Delany's fragmentary narrative technique calls into question assumptions about agency and continuity. He realizes that utopian spaces ought not to be described in systematic prose, and they retain or even increase their political potency when they stretch or contort language, techniques Delany was then also experimenting with in his science fiction.[15]

Perhaps provoked by Scott's challenge, Delany continued his formal experimentation (now including unconventional typography and photography) in his third memoir, in which he makes explicit that his principal aim is challenging domination, not celebrating identity and individual agency. In *Times Square Red, Times Square Blue* he looks back on the decades when pornography movie theaters thrived in midtown Manhattan from the perspective of a moment when Mayor Rudolph Giuliani was forcing the last of the theaters to close. In his preface, Delany writes, "The polemical passion here is forward-looking, not nostalgic, however respectful it is of a past we may find useful for grounding future possibility." He wants his readers to imagine new futures, futures impermissible under the current economic, racial, and sexual regime. These futures are partially accessible to us; we catch glimmers of them that are quickly smothered but that still motivate—not only one group, gay men, but all as we seek freedom.[16]

While popular culture imagines pornographic theaters as seedy sites where moral degenerates congregate, Delany describes a predominantly working-class but hugely varied clientele: "Playwrights, carpenters, opera singers, telephone repair men, stockbrokers, guys on welfare, guys with trust funds, guys on crutches." Only in the theaters did Delany ever have an extended conversation with a Hasidic Jew. The world of the theaters can appear rough, but it is a space where many sorts of people may negotiate relations and intimacy with each other. The theaters are dilapidated but functional; there are homeless men and mentally ill men, but they are not a danger to others. There are men who offer sex for money, but they are a minority. While popular culture imagines the sex that occurs in such theaters to be brief, random, and emotionless, Delany describes a wide variety of encounters, from the brief and purely sexual to those that involved long personal conversations to those that launched long-term relationships. The theater was a place for intimacy and actual relationships—"But, like all sane relationships, they also had limits." Sometimes Delany would go out and bring back a sandwich or drink for a new acquaintance, sometimes there would be an invitation home. Sometimes, after sex, they would talk for hours, sometimes not at all. Most of the time, when one theatergoer proposed sex to another, the answer was no; this was accepted without hurt feelings.[17]

The first half of *Times Square Red, Times Square Blue* offers stories illuminating the world of the theaters; the second half offers a theory. What the theaters create, Delany suggests, is a zone of contact, not community. There are no criteria for membership, no fixed norms to be followed. Rather, it is a space where people radically different from each other in race, class, and occupation can encounter one another. What Delany finds in the theaters he also finds, less intensely, in urban life writ large: in line at the grocery store, at the post office, in the street, at the park. Contact gives cities their vitality. But the forces of domination are set on restricting spaces of contact in the name of "safety." (Delany is particularly concerned with economic domination by wealthy developers and their clients, but he recognizes that race and economics are entangled.) Those on the side of domination favor a different sort of social encounter, one Delany labels "network," where people of the same class congregate in pursuit of limited opportunities for advancement: gallery openings, conferences, gyms. Network reinforces structures of domination, fueled by the elusive promise of rewards. Contact offers actual rewards, but they are unpredictable. Delany recalls acquiring a vacuum cleaner at a copy center, and connecting an acquaintance from the pornographic theaters with a job in publishing.

From his first memoir to his last, Delany becomes more rigorously apophatic. He moves from speaking of a physical space without domination, the commune, to describing shifting sites of encounter where we can find a foretaste of freedom. And that foretaste is pure potential: each encounter may yield a pleasant surprise, or it may not. In a world where desires are so thoroughly contaminated, the futures Delany imagines and samples feature desire freed. "I learned to move within the circle of other people's desire, and be at ease as I generated my own. And I would strike one of my senses before I would part with that knowledge." Here is dignity: a vision of desires indomitable motivating struggle against forces of domination.[18]

Martin Luther King, Jr., is the paradigm of an American prophet, denouncing injustice and rallying the masses for action. Michael Walzer has argued that the prophet's vocation is to name the ways current social practices mismatch the deeply held values of a community, values implicit in that community's history and culture. George Shulman, using King and James Baldwin as examples, importantly adds that in prophecy, part of a community that is present but unrepresented, erased from a community's self-understanding, makes its voice heard, forcing the community to reassess what its core values really are and what new shape it must take to live up to those values.[19]

But the era for prophecy on this grand model is over. Black activists today talk about the need to challenge domination not only in the world but in the movements that struggle against domination. This means challenging leaders who, intentionally or not, dominate movement organizations. Instead of purging all leaders, activists call for "leaderful" movements, activist cultures that cultivate the capacity for leadership in each participant and find each one a leadership role. Given this shift in activist culture, is there any room left for prophetic figures, even one very different from Martin Luther King, Jr.?[20]

Perhaps Delany offers a model of what a Black prophet looks like in this new era, a corrective that aligns prophecy with Black dignity. Unlike Walzer's prophets, Delany does not pretend to synthesize a history and culture, distill its values, or pass judgment; nor, unlike Shulman's prophets, does he speak on behalf of those present but unrepresented. Delany stands not at the center of social movements but on the edges. He concerns himself primarily with imagining futures. These cannot be reduced to gay or Black or working-class futures.

They are futures after all domination is done away with, after the end of the world. But they are not post-racial or pan-sexual futures. They are told at particular moments in time, attentive to the complex texture of the world, targeted at systems of domination that are especially vulnerable to challenge. Where King's stories of hope are nurtured in churches, stolid institutions with noble histories, for Delany hope is nurtured in fleeting sites of contact—youth communes, gay bathhouses, pornographic movie theaters. Perhaps the role of prophet today, like the sites of contact of which Delany writes, exists fleetingly, at the edges, and ultimately in our imaginations.

6

Black Magic

Black Christian clergy are not front and center in today's racial justice movement. Talk of Jesus and God is more likely to be part of an expletive than a speech. On the other hand, spiritual talk and spiritual practice saturate movement spaces, online and in person. The hashtag Black magic condenses and evokes this diffuse spirituality. Rather than being led by God's representatives on earth, Black folks understand divine power as manifesting inside us as we struggle. Religion suggests institutions; magic suggests the extraordinary power of individuals. It can be easy to dismiss movement spirituality as fuzzy New Ageism, but it is deeply connected with the commitment to Black dignity. If the world gripped by interlocking systems of domination were all there is, struggle would be futile. Black dignity, performed in struggle, is made possible by spiritual commitments.

In a 2016 interview with Krista Tippett, public radio's resident spirituality fangirl, Black Lives Matter co-founder Patrisse Cullors reflected on the transformation that happens to people when they commit to Black struggle: a spiritual light begins to glow inside them. Cullors, who majored in religion and philosophy at UCLA, founded Dignity and Power Now, a Los Angeles–based grassroots organization struggling to end mass incarceration. In her conversation with Tippett, she recalled her great-grandfather, an American Indian medicine man who taught her the importance of healing as spiritual work. Given the continual attacks on Black bodies and souls, healing in a broad sense becomes essential for Black survival. It is also essential for Black self-determination: state intervention and state violence are often justified as redress to harms inflicted by and on Black folks. The prison system is being shrunk, but the end of the prison will not mean the end of domination; we will still inflict vicious harms on each other that require repair. New practices for healing harms must be found.[1]

Instead of receiving religion from a single, often Christian and male authority, and instead of holding membership in a formal religious community, many Black youths—like growing numbers of Americans generally—identify more with spirituality than religion. They become spiritual bricoleurs, picking and choosing useful elements of different religious and spiritual traditions. This follows a long history of Afro-Atlantic religiosity, born during the Middle Passage, responding to unspeakable suffering by selectively drawing on beliefs and practices from Christianity, African traditional religions, and Native American traditions. Some activists, identifying Christianity with racial, gender, and sexual domination, turn away from it completely. Cullors, for example, observes Ifá, an African traditional religion of the Yoruba people. Regardless of activists' affiliations, Black protests in our era are filled with spiritual symbols: prayer, altars, burning sage, the invocation of ancestors. Ifá iconography in particular shows up repeatedly. Following Los Angeles police officers' 2014 shooting of Ezell Ford, for example, protesters gathered at the mayor's house wearing all white, after the clothing worn during Ifá sacred rites. The music video for D Smoke's anthem of Black dignity, "Black Habits," features a group of Black women wearing all white, holding hands in a circle in what is unmistakably an African-derived religious ceremony.[2]

Cullors observes, "I don't believe Black people ever get respite and so we have become incredibly intelligent about how we come to peace." Struggle is continuous, and not by choice. By "peace," Cullors does not mean a break from struggle; she means coming to terms with the continuity of struggle. Spirituality and the arts promise peace in this sense. For her culminating MFA project, in 2019, Cullors created *Respite, Reprieve, and Healing: An Evening of Cleansing.* This performance, to which all audience members were asked to wear white, was meant not to entertain but to initiate performers and observers into a collective practice aimed at self-determination. In the opening scene, what looks like a rope for lynching turns out to be a rope for hair binding: the collective transforms a symbol of a profane rite of whiteness into a symbol for a sacred rite of Blackness. Cullors describes Black hair care as a spiritual practice, both "baptismal" and, in the Ifá tradition, linking humans to each other and to God—but a practice that is often performed only privately. In *Respite, Reprieve, and Healing,* as in contemporary Black activist culture more broadly, sacred rites are made public, gathering community and orienting them toward struggle.[3]

Religious studies scholar Biko Gray analyzes the presence of spiritual talk and practice in Black Lives Matter–affiliated spaces by pointing to the way anti-Blackness forecloses possibility. It is necessary to say "Black lives matter" because Black lives are treated as if they do not. We still live in the afterlives of slavery; we are treated as object rather than person, disposable, susceptible to premature death. Integrated into laws, habits, and hearts, anti-Blackness makes Black life impossible. According to Gray, activists' "vision of Blackness as irreducibly sacred" gives the lie to the impossibility of Black life. The varied spiritual language and practices associated with the movement flow out of this sense of sacred Blackness. Cullors goes further, asserting that the sacredness of Black life is not simply a fact affirmed but an ongoing struggle, "part of a larger fight" that we all wage to live in a world bent on denying life—a fight "which is deeply spiritual."[4]

Like masters, bosses, and kings, gods dominate. By definition, a god has extraordinary powers and arbitrarily intervenes in the world in ways that are sometimes inscrutable to humans. Modes of domination tend to merge; the Christian God was long pictured as a white man. Struggling against domination, then, includes struggling against gods. On the other hand, what if gods mark the limits of the world? Secularism—originally worldliness, now an ideology that excludes the otherworldly—tells us to ignore the limits of the world; this is all there is. If our world is infested with domination, and domination thrives by making it seem as if there is no alternative, then secularism is a tool of domination. It cuts off the possibility of thinking and acting otherwise. Talk of gods reopens that possibility.[5]

Scholars and practitioners of religion know that nothing can be said a priori about religion and domination. Religious practices and traditions are complex, sometimes complicit in domination, sometimes challenging it. The spirituality of contemporary Black activist circles aims to demarcate those religious practices, images, and ideas that challenge domination. But we must take care not to instrumentalize spirituality as simply a tool aiding struggle. If spirituality aids struggle, it is at a deeper level. Spirituality refuses the limited set of possibilities for struggle and reminds practitioners that there are possibilities beyond those they have imagined—aiding struggle by potentially transforming the mode of struggle.

At first it seems as though there is a zero-sum logic of oppressor and oppressed, master and slave. In that logic, each victory for the slave in search of her freedom is a loss for the master. If spirituality were a tool, it would help slaves in this struggle. But this is not the logic of domination. Both master and slave play parts in its dynamic. Both have their perceptions, feelings, thoughts, and actions distorted by domination. To believe oneself more human than another requires a grotesquely warped image of one's own humanity, just as being treated as less than human grotesquely warps one's humanity. Europeans, whites, men, straight people, able-bodied people: all, given the superior positions they enjoy in systems of domination, live deeply distorted lives. Domination creates the horizon of possibility, including the possibility of struggle against itself. As the master and slave struggle, they cannot veer from the scripts made available by the system of domination. Successful systems of domination have a noose-like hold: the more one struggles, the tighter their grip. Resistance is futile. Spiritual practices demonstrate that the world does not have the last word, even when it seems as though domination is strengthened by struggle.

Put another way, we do not live in laboratory conditions, in a world consisting only of master and slave, or of a class of masters and another of slaves. We live in a world of interlocking systems of domination. But neither is the world the sum of all systems of domination, nor is a person's existence defined only by the sum of her entanglements in systems of domination. Some historians and anthropologists would have us look down rather than up: elite discourse may, in fact, be entirely captured by domination. But if we look at ordinary people, and at practices rather than words, we find domination stretched, fragmented, incomplete. On the plantation, slaves may say yes and no to their masters at the appropriate times in the Big House, but out in the fields, the story is quite different. You hear freedom songs and see crops pilfered. The more domination one endures, the more absurd domination's strategies of control and concealment become. To those who are most poor, it is most obvious that the economy is rigged by the rich; to Black women, the machinations of anti-Blackness and patriarchy can appear crystal clear. It is only the bourgeoisie who are fooled, who cannot see domination operative in the world or themselves as beneficiaries of domination, as masters. If domination freezes souls like ice on a lake, there is liquid water underneath. Movement spirituality turns our attention to that liquid water, whether it is through Christian liberation theology's identification of God with "the least of these" or through recovering cultural-religious practices of African ancestors that were partially erased during the Middle Passage.

While this account connects spirituality to the quantity of domination, there is another sense in which spirituality is connected to the quality of domination. Domination involves the arbitrary exercise of one person's will over another. Note how this arbitrariness already involves a certain spontaneity, unpredictability. For there to be domination, social practices and norms cannot offer an exhaustive account of the human condition. Domination is not just about poor socialization; it grows out of a frustrated desire to reduce our humanity to worldly terms. If only people would do what they ought to do, stay in their place, do as they are told. Investment in and naturalization of domination create an illusion of safety and security that is, in reality, blocked by the antinomies of being a human in the world but irreducible to the world. Just as the arbitrary exercise of the will that flows from our humanity gives rise to domination, it also thwarts domination. We are never truly at home in the world. From the world's perspective, we have a tendency to strike out against it, against the social norms we are prescribed. This behavior can seem to be erratic, or a flight of fancy, or temporary insanity. But as we begin to realize that those social norms are formed and fueled by domination, our discontent focuses on a target. Once domination is taken away, we can be free: we can realize our humanity. And we realize our humanity, in its irreducibility to worldly terms, as we struggle against domination. This is spiritual work: probing our souls and directing their unimaginable energy. Christian theologians may describe this as the image of God in the human; other spiritual practitioners may describe it as a life force. False religions (of whiteness, patriarchy, colonialism) sacralize the arbitrary will of some while offering the duplicitous promise of safety and security to all.

If we combine the quantitative and qualitative accounts of domination and spirituality, we arrive at Black magic. Those most affected by domination are in the best position to exercise their inherently human capacity to perform creatively, unpredictably, and in a way that challenges systems of domination. Competing with this capacity is the debilitating pressure those systems exercise. Out of this combustible mixture comes something magical, Black excellence, the extraordinary and seemingly inexplicable performances of some Black artists, singers, scientists, and political leaders. Whereas well-acculturated whites can achieve competence with little resistance by doing what they are supposed to do, that pathway is rarely available to Blacks. Those who can overcome the barriers are often capable of excellence rather than competence, meaning a performance that has the potential to transform a social practice, to set new standards for what counts as competence. When patriarchy and anti-Blackness intersect, we find an especially combustible potential labeled Black girl magic.

While Black magic as it circulates in the racial justice movement today is a new formulation of Black spirituality, it fits neatly in line with the work of earlier generations of Black activist-intellectuals or at least the sharpest representatives of those earlier generations who understood struggle to be fueled by spirituality. It may seem as if those who turned away from Christianity toward supposedly traditional African religious practice, as in strands of Black cultural nationalism and the Negritude movement, turned away from spirituality's horizon-opening power in favor of manufactured nostalgia, but Aimé Césaire reminds us that this need not be the case. Similarly, it may seem as if Black Christian liberation theologians are hopelessly tethered to white, colonial forms of religious thought, practice, and institutions, but in fact a theologian like James Cone embraces Black dignity and resources today's struggle in much the same way as Césaire. The distance between Christianity and magic is not as great you would think.

Césaire's narrative poem *Notebook of a Return to a Native Land* describes a journey of Black formation that is also deformation. It explores the way magic interrupts Black life, occasioning dignity, and the way religion is manipulated to control Black life, occasioning indignity. Césaire, who composed it on returning to Martinique after studying in Paris, places spirituality at the center of his narrative. He contrasts religions false and true: during his childhood, neither teachers nor priests could get the young narrator to speak, no matter how much force they used, because he knew he desired something illegible to them, outside their shared world, constituted as it was by racial and colonial domination. They tried to teach him the law, the Ten Commandments, but he was lost in a "hunger buried in the depths of Hunger." He longed for something he could not articulate; together with his classmates, family, and neighbors, he longed for something colonial rulers and their law could not provide.[6]

Christmas, away from the enforcers of the colonial order, was a magical time, a reminder that the colonial order was less exhaustive than it seemed. Then it appeared as if the Black community could flourish free of domination in "an unimposing little church that would benevolently make room for the laughter, the whispers, the secrets, the love talk, the gossip and the guttural cacophony of a plucky singer." From anticipation and preparation to pulsing collectivity to ecstasy, "ALLELUIA / KYRIE ELEISON," the celebration of Christ's birth marked a foretaste of a time to come, a time when all would share, with Christ, in genuine freedom. At the height of ecstasy, freedom was not only an intellectual matter; it was felt bodily: "Not only do the mouths sing, but the hands, the feet, the buttocks, the genitals, and your entire being . . . [liquefy] into sounds, voices and rhythm."[7]

Christmas promises freedom, and then it comes to an end. The celebrants are still poor Black folks living under colonial rule. After Christmas, "You don't know how to dispose of your aborted dreams, the river of life desperately torpid." Boredom returns for some, fits of anger for others, rat-filled houses and bad air for many. For Césaire, both the colonizer's religion, inflicted as law, and the spiritual ecstasy of that religion turned inside out, from mind to body, are inadequate responses to the situation in which he and his people find themselves. The colonizer's religion is in unconcealed alliance with the forces of domination ("the bread and the wine of complicity"); spiritual ecstasy purports to open new futures but actually leaves domination intact. Christmas stokes the hunger of those who celebrate it, putting in relief systems of domination—"the joy of former times making me aware of my present poverty."[8]

Césaire leaves his island, driven by the desire he cannot yet name. When he returns, equipped now to give voice to his people's grievances, he fancies himself their spokesman. But he worries that this stance makes him a spectator to suffering while turning his people into a circus attraction. He finds himself in but no longer of his former world, and his hunger remains unsated. Then he realizes how to find brotherhood. It is with those Blacks who suffer around the world, from France to England to the United States. In shared suffering, shared blood, he finds an answer to his longings. The world he thought he inhabited was false. It appeared reasonable and safe, but that was a ruse to conceal the violence of racial and colonial domination. The necessary response is to reject the logic of that world—not for a moment of ecstasy but for ongoing struggle. "Because we hate you and your reason," he writes to the forces of domination, "we claim kinship with dementia praecox, with the flaming madness of persistent cannibalism." It is through madness rather than reason that clarity can be achieved and we can see, feel, and know rightly.[9]

With this embrace of madness, Césaire claims his descent from others who have been dismissed as mad, particularly Africans. European rule and religion must be abandoned.

I declare my crimes and that there is nothing to say in my
defense.
Dances. Idols. An Apostate. I too
I have assassinated God with my laziness with my words
with my gestures with my obscene songs.

His poem becomes an incantation, a prayer to the African spirits
punctuated by the repeated cry, "voum rooh oh." With that spell, he
claims power over nature, power over the world, envisioning a time
when he and his people will live without domination. Instead of a
respectable prophet leading his people, Césaire aspires to be a conjurer, marshalling those in the shadow of domination, living and
dead, to destroy and rebuild the world with spiritual power.[10]

The moment in *Notebook of a Return to a Native Land* when
Césaire embraced shared Black suffering, madness, and African conjuring gave rise to a literary movement, Negritude, celebrating African heritage, but it was not the end of Césaire's poem. One final act
remains. The poet realizes that his aspiration to be a conjurer and to
find ancestors in Africa and brothers among Blacks around the world
was a product of his own desire to dominate. He too sought safety
and comfort, control of his surroundings—now through madness
and demonic powers. Césaire realizes this when he encounters a particularly downtrodden Black man on the streetcar, a man whose physical and spiritual being is the opposite of the African nobility Césaire
has embraced. Césaire's confidence in his own dignity, which he understands in the ancient, European, aristocratic sense, makes him
look down upon the poor man. Reflecting on that reaction, he realizes
he must change his outlook.

The position Césaire arrives at in the poem's final stanzas acknowledges shared suffering and ancestry without glorifying it. Africans need not be celebrated for their greatness; they could be honored

in their defeat. What matters, at the end of the day, is humanity, not inventions or explorations or even heroic resistance. Césaire celebrates those who live in right relation to their land and their fellows, "who yield, captivated, to the essence of things," who are "indifferent to conquering, but playing the game of the world." He commends attention, undistorted by the forces of domination that contaminate our perception. This includes attention to oneself, to one's feelings, to joy, love, and grief, so that they too may be felt rightly, undistorted. To see and feel without distortion is impossible in this world; Césaire therefore resorts to prayer. He asks for the strength of character needed to attend rightly to world and self, capable of continually purging those forces that distort. He asks to be like a pirogue, one of the small boats used by the indigenous people of the Caribbean to move between islands. A pirogue is gently guided so that its movements at once struggle with the sea and are in harmony with it, the boat's course directed by its skilled occupant. This movement of the pirogue, which Césaire prays may become the shape of his life, he labels "the sacred dance." After attempting several false forms of religion, he has finally settled on an account of spirituality that is aligned with struggle.[11]

While suspicion of institutionalized Christianity pervades today's racial justice movement, a number of activists identify with strands of progressive Christianity, particularly liberation theology. For example, Bree Newsome, who entered the national spotlight when she removed the Confederate flag from the South Carolina capitol following the massacre of Black churchgoers in Charleston, sees her activism flowing from faith in a Jesus who sides with the oppressed. She was led up that flagpole by the Holy Spirit. Newsome believes God listens to the prayers of the most marginalized: "I know that he heard my great-great-grandmother in South Carolina when she was praying for her

children to be free, and we're going to keep praying until we're all free."
With confidence that God is on her side, she can struggle fearlessly
against the seemingly insurmountable forces of racial domination.[12]

Osagyefo Uhuru Sekou was born in St. Louis in 1971, became a
minister, and spent years as an itinerant speaker, singer, filmmaker,
and activist. Early in the 2014 Ferguson uprising, he returned to his
hometown to organize and inspire the rapidly politicizing youths who
turned out every night to protest Michael Brown's death, in itself and
as a symbol of police violence and anti-Blackness. He was arrested
multiple times, once in front of the Ferguson Police Department at an
interfaith pray-in that he helped organize. Despite his clerical collar
and Christian phraseology, Sekou reflects, "I'm not terribly hopeful
for the church. I think queer, black, poor women are the church's salvation. They don't need to get saved. The church needs to get saved."
He sees those who are most marginalized as a source of moral authority, and the truths proclaimed by the church need to be accountable to
those struggling on the margins. Two years after Ferguson, Sekou released "The Revolution Has Come," a gospel-blues anthem mapping
the Christian temporality of Resurrection onto the struggle against
domination. "What a time to be alive," he belts, "when we stand up /
we've already won." Organizing against domination is itself a practice
of freedom, not just a precursor to freedom. As Sekou puts it, "I understand the gospel to affirm black dignity and self-determination."[13]

Christianity is often dismissed as either overly moralistic in this
world or distracted by the next. The strands of Christianity embraced
by Sekou, Newsome, and other activists reject both moralizing and
otherworldliness. They see the story of Jesus as dramatizing the way
the forces of domination seem to have a stranglehold on the world,
but they believe God will not let that happen. Appearing in human
form as a poor, brown-skinned Palestinian Jew, God is persecuted by
the forces of empire and their privileged local allies. First W. E. B. Du

Bois, then the Black liberation theologians James Cone and Kelly Brown Douglas responded to lynchings by retelling the gospel narrative in the American South, making clear how the forces of racial domination are one with the forces of domination that crucified Jesus. Belief in God means belief that those forces ultimately fail. Believers gathered together for action, whether that is prayer, song, or standing with the poor and marginalized, are animated by the confidence that they will prevail—which is to say, they are led by the Spirit. "In the act of worship itself," Cone writes, "the experience of liberation becomes a constituent of the community's being."[14]

Black Christians embracing this perspective look at the way domination conceals itself in idolatry, promising satisfaction through worship of worldly things that will inevitably disappoint. The task of Christians, then, is not only to gather together to shape collective rage and love into on-the-ground struggle but also to sharpen their critical instincts. As a group, telling stories of religious struggle from the past and holding up examples of struggle in the present, they resist the temptation to orient life around the quest for security and safety. Only God, in whom we can participate through struggle, can offer a guarantee of security and safety; money and privilege offer but a false copy.

Put another way, the liberation theology aligned with Black activism is deeply committed to negative theology, the belief that the only true things that we can say about God are what God is not. Because God is wholly other than the world, any attempt to use the world's words will get God wrong, will in fact be a projection of worldly interests onto the divine: idolatry. Hence the need to employ song and stories to orient us toward God. Happily, humans were created in the image of God, a similitude most intense in Jesus, who *is* God, but impossible to capture in concepts. While the forces of domination that infest the world conspire to make us forget that something in us is irreducible to worldly terms, Christian communities attend to those embers, gathering and oxygenating them, so that we may more clearly recognize who we are beyond what we are. This process necessarily looks and sounds bizarre from the world's perspective. As the critic Ashon Crawley has noted, at their purest, Black sociality and Pentecostal sociality have much in common. They employ language, noise, and bodily movements that are unintelligible to the world, transgress national and class divides, and conjure radically different futures that put in relief the demonic forces at work in the present world.[15]

When Black Christians emphasize the negative aspect of their theology in service of liberation, it opens possibilities for deep interfaith collaboration. James Cone noticed the close alignment between the political-theological views of Martin Luther King, Jr., and those of Malcolm X. "The depth of any religious commitment," he argues, "should be judged by one's commitment to justice for humanity, using the liberation activity of human beings as the lens through which one sees God." By this criterion, both King and Malcolm are models for Christians—where the focus on liberation activity supersedes any judgment based on the content of their religious creeds or their personal morality.[16]

This tendency to focus on actions and political orientations rather than creeds left Black liberation theology vulnerable to co-optation during the era of multiculturalism. Critics charged that privileging the category "Black" erased the intersectional nature of oppression. Black women, queer Blacks, and immigrant Blacks all face their own particular difficulties, and God is on the side of each. Where Black liberation theology had been closely aligned with the Black power movement, the era of multiculturalism changed it from a political theology into a contextual theology. According to the latter, different marginalized communities each have their own ways of worshipping, reading the Bible, and speaking of their religious experience, based on the particular forms of oppression to which they must respond. While this move seemed to decenter white, Europe-focused Christianity in favor of a rainbow of ethnic and cultural Christianities, in fact it ceded power from God to the world. Specific ethnic and cultural groupings, brought into being by forces of domination, were given ultimate religious authority. To take but one example, for Womanism, a label for Black feminist Christianity, the experience of Black women became the ultimate criterion of truth. But that experience is worldly, not otherworldly; it is shaped by dynamics of domination, and elevating its authority deprives Christians of the ability to cleave the image of God from its distortions. What seemed like a pluralization of Christian liberation theologies was actually an abandonment of Christianity's power to thwart systems of domination through the imperative of collective struggle.[17]

It is almost too obvious to need saying: racial justice activism today affirms the value of Black life. Packed into that affirmation are spiritual commitments not only regarding the image of the divine in the human but also the way we ought to relate to death. Ruth Wilson Gilmore defines racism as "the state-sanctioned or extralegal production and exploitation of group-differentiated vulnerability to premature death." In other words, the cornerstone of anti-Blackness is untimely Black death. Domination thrives on that possibility and uses it to secure its grip: from death in the hold of a slave ship to death from exhaustion or violence on the plantation to death at the hands of the lynch mob—to death at the hands of the state, whether officially through capital punishment, unofficially through police violence, or slowly, as Black bodies and psyches are worn down by environmental and economic conditions.[18]

All human life ends in death, and any human life may end in tragically premature death. The world dominates us, exercising arbitrary power over our lives. That domination is only intensified in the relationship between master and slave: in the primal scene of domination, the master can at any moment take the life of his slave without having to answer for it. There will be no legal consequences, and there will be no grief. To say that Black lives matter means that premature Black death requires public accountability and public mourning. Vulnerability to premature death makes survival the necessary focus of Black life. To affirm the value of Black life means to open up the possibility of Black life beyond survival: life that is rich and creative, flourishing. As Patrisse Cullors puts it, "We've lived in a place that has literally allowed for us to believe and center only black death. We've forgotten how to imagine black life." But how can there be flourishing in life if death is inevitable, if domination is indestructible? This is where spirituality comes in, with its insistence that domination and death cannot have the last word, are not the ultimate authorities on life. There can be life beyond death: this we must believe.[19]

Overcoming death and embracing new life: it sounds like a mystical, abstract, perhaps anaesthetizing proposition. Does it not require an outlandish belief in the afterlife? Recall the temporality evoked by Osagyefo Sekou in his song "The Revolution Has Come." When we struggle in our present world, we have a foretaste of freedom, of a world beyond domination located on the eschatological horizon. Struggling against domination opens possibilities for flourishing. The fact of death does not go away, but its significance begins to dissolve. Sekou invokes his grandmother, who sang, "I'm too busy working for my Jesus / I ain't got time to die." The world freed from domination lies on the other side of an unbridgeable divide, but that is only how it appears from the domination-filled world. As we participate in struggle, we participate in freedom, and the significance of the divide between present and future worlds fades.[20]

James Cone makes this point in a Christian idiom. "Because we know that death has been conquered, we are truly free to be human in history." For him, the life and death of Jesus confirm that death has been conquered, but it is also confirmed in the urban rebellions of the late 1960s that prompted him to formulate a Black theology. Blacks came to realize that if domination has the last word, life is not worth living. Vulnerability to premature death clarified the matter: "For blacks death is not really a future reality; it is a part of their everyday existence. They see death every time they see whites." Continually at risk of death, Blacks can realize that it makes sense to struggle, even if struggle means risking death. To struggle is to reject the hold of domination, to embrace new life, and to begin to realize our humanity. As Cone puts it, "The rebellion in the cities is not a conscious organized attempt of black people to take over; it is an attempt to say *yes* to their own dignity even in death." Rebellion, he suggests, makes Blacks "indifferent toward death" because the freedom we taste in struggle is so sweet.[21]

In a spiritual rather than religious idiom, Aimé Césaire also embraces Black life after death. When he returns from his studies in Paris, he finds life in his island clouded by death. Not grand death, but mundane death caused by small-minded colonizers. Death (and life) on Martinique is ultimately futile; he is struck by its "dazzling pettiness." But after he comes to realize that the seemingly trivial Black death in his small island is connected with Black death around the world, and Black struggles around the world—"marshes of putrid blood"—the meaning of death begins to change. Vulnerability to death binds Blacks together and, embracing the power of Blackness and African ancestors, Césaire learns "to charm snakes" and "to conjure the dead." He learns how to exercise power over death, in a sense, to dominate death along with the rest of the natural world. Again, this is not the end of the story. Césaire tells of the captain of a slave ship who, merely to break the tedium of the long voyage, decides to hang the largest of his Black cargo. As the enslaved man is unshackled, put on his feet, and brought from the ship's hold up to the deck, he briefly tastes life without domination. The act of standing up, Césaire repeats over and over, gives freedom. With that realization, the cloud of death over Black life lifts. Everything is not better; the facts of the world are the same. But now life can be lived zealously. Césaire concludes, "And the great black hole where a moon ago I wanted to drown / It is there I will now fish."[22]

Césaire constantly attends to the particularities of the natural world. When Black life in the Caribbean is shadowed by death, the natural environment conspires with colonialism and capitalism to dominate. Volcanoes, waves, and sun exercise arbitrary power over his island's inhabitants, and it seems as though the people will expire— "Nothing will be left but a tepid bubbling pecked at by sea birds." The attention to oneself and other humans that Césaire commends, made possible by his realization of domination's power and its limits, extends to the natural world. Blacks have a particular privilege in this regard, he suggests, with the violence of domination offering lessons in attention to place, flora, and fauna, and the ways they are misperceived. Just as Blacks can lose the sense of death as existential threat through struggle and attention, all of us can lose the sense that the (equally inevitable) end of the human species is an existential threat. Rather than make us complacent, this realization brings clarity to the struggle against all forms of domination, each of which is linked to human domination over the natural environment. Attending to the natural world is a spiritual practice. Retaining that sense of spirituality makes us rightly suspicious both of moralizing rhetoric about the environment and purported technical solutions to the climate crisis. Moralizing and scientism are genres of domination employed to trap listeners into choosing among the options on the table—a table set by domination—when they should overturn the table and imagine otherwise. Precisely what the language and practices of struggle look like once these obstacles are avoided cannot be determined a priori. Struggle flows from attention to the particulars of people and place, mindful of the complex and shifting nature of domination as well as its incapacity ever to be complete: spirituality defines that dimension of being human that domination can never capture. Black spirituality gives us the confidence to struggle with discipline and precision in a context where the odds seem impossible. In such contexts, Black magic promises felicitous surprises.[23]

7

I Believe in the Revolution

Three years before Trayvon Martin was killed, five years before Michael Brown's death, a twenty-two-year-old Black man named Oscar Grant was shot from behind by a white police officer in Oakland. Hundreds protested in the streets, primarily Black youths; some set cars and dumpsters on fire and broke windows. Oakland mayor Ron Dellums, a Black septuagenarian and former congressman whose progressive credentials included spotlighting American war crimes in Vietnam, organizing opposition to the apartheid regime in South Africa, and inclusion on Richard Nixon's enemies list, attempted to calm the crowd. The response: a chant of "Fuck Obama and fuck Dellums." It was not the time for reform. It was the time for revolution.[1]

Black activist and minister Lynice Pinkard argued that the white police officer who killed Grant was inhabiting the role of plantation overseer. He was ostensibly serving the people but actually serving the master. Pinkard is careful not to identify white people as masters; it is systems of domination that occupy a position of mastery. Those systems live inside people, including the police officer but also Oscar Grant—and all of us. They try to take hold of our souls, but with only partial success, leading to affective tumult and disorder. "The plantation of this world is so *within* us," Pinkard asserts, that the struggle for freedom also plays out inside us. "We are always being pulled this way and that by unconscious forms of racism and classism, by heterosexism (a spawn of sexism), and by ageism, ableism, corporatism, nationalism, globalism, militarism, and capitalism—overarching structures of domination working in tandem." It often seems easiest just to go where we are being pulled. Doing so feels natural. That is the genius of domination's self-concealment.[2]

Pinkard fully supports the youths who took to the streets in the wake of Grant's death, but she believes their revolutionary ambitions were not grand enough. The struggle against plantation masters and overseers, the struggle against police violence, and the struggle against domination within ourselves are all of a kind. Each requires a decisive response. According to Pinkard, the fitting response, at the level of our souls, is "revolutionary suicide," a concept she borrows from Black Panther leader Huey P. Newton. The forces of domination have such a hold on our ways of thinking, feeling, and acting that to move toward freedom we must excise a part of ourselves. The goal of this work is not personal liberation but preparation for joining the collective struggle. Unless we do the proper work on ourselves, we will overlook the way domination operates in the world, or misidentify it, or respond inappropriately. Domination infects the soul by preying on our desire for safety and security. It promises an orderly world where we can count on getting what we need. It makes us ask, if we do not live on the master's plantation, how will we find the food and shelter we need to survive? If we do not live in this particular suburb and send our children to that particular school, how will we assure that their lives will be safe and secure?[3]

Anxieties about safety and security are rooted deep in our humanity; to be human means not to be at home in the world. These anxieties are exploited by particular systems of domination. Using churches, schools, laws, and the arts as intermediaries, systems of domination form us to find comfort in white suburbia, or in institutions of Black respectability like sororities and fraternities, or in makeup and tight dresses. We cling to the habits and practices smuggled into our lives by domination, but they destroy us. Not in themselves as individual practices, but because our affective investment in them, as guarantors of our safety and security, is also affective investment in systems of domination whether we imagine ourselves in the position of master or slave. Domination wills the death of us all: rendering some vulnerable to premature death but also, even more significantly, casting the shadow of death over every life, making lives lifeless. Yes, we are hurtling toward climate disaster, but Pinkard charges that already today, billions are living in such disharmony with themselves and the world that what they have can hardly be called life.

Once we recognize this cataclysmic situation, Pinkard argues, we must perform the therapeutic work on ourselves necessary to identify and manage our need for safety and security so that it cannot be exploited. Then we can purge from our lives those beliefs and practices that we thought would guarantee safety and security. The goal is not to become less racist, or less sexist, or to share your wealth; it is to become a new person, unrecognizable if measured by *what* you are but in harmony with *who* you are. The bundle of practices that make us respectable and righteous in the eyes of the world must be sacrificed in order to have a new life born of struggle. Hollow dignity, attaching to nobility, must be traded in for true dignity, performed when we confront domination in our souls and in the world—as we impossibly strive to renounce the ways in which we are shaped by whiteness, patriarchy, ableism, capitalism, and much else.

This therapeutic work takes faith. It takes perseverance in the face of impossible odds and uncountable setbacks. Its yield will always seem uncertain. As Pinkard puts it, "Whether one feels this tearing and release—a crucifixion and resurrection of the self—as the work of demons or of angels depends on one's openness and commitment to transformation and revolution." Belief comes before evidence: commitment to struggle cannot follow from the fruits of struggle. A leap of faith is necessary, but it is not simply existential. It is embedded in community. As Alicia Garza wrote in her Facebook post founding Black Lives Matter, "Stop giving up on black life. Black people, I will *never* give up on us. *Never*." Just as the desire for safety and security can leave souls susceptible to domination, the sense of comfort provided by a community can make it possible to believe in that community beyond reason. Often, commitment to a community coincides with domination: the community at issue is understood in a way that is structured, for example, by nationalism, patriarchy, or white supremacy. But because Blackness is so tightly (though not absolutely) identified with slavery, faith in Black people can develop into faith in the struggle against domination as such. While Blackness is often misunderstood, and the comfort it offers to Blacks is sometimes unhelpful, Black folks are in a unique position to draw on our communities to fuel and guide struggle.[4]

Whereas previous chapters meditate on key concepts of today's racial justice movement, this chapter explores a political orientation. If anti-Blackness so thoroughly infects the world, revolutionary change is needed. Dignity entails revolution. But revolution today means something quite different than in the 1960s, or in the nineteenth century. It still means uprooting systems of domination, but today it is essentially negative and plural: against domination rather than for a particular configuration of state or society, pursued collectively and diversely as those most affected by domination organize together. Revolution today is a bottom-up affair. Activists have a healthy suspicion of those who present themselves, or are presented by the media, as movement leaders (and as intellectuals), believing instead that clarity, wisdom, and energy are to be found at the grass roots. Even the women who coined #BlackLivesMatter, thus achieving celebrity status, have attracted suspicion. Envisioning a revolution from below requires probing the thought and practice of those who claim to be revolutionaries today as well as their historical antecedents. Earlier Black revolutionaries help bring clarity to today's murky language, and the knowledge gleaned from today's movement guides us to the revolutionaries of the past who best avoided the temptations of top-down thinking and practice.

Many young Black activists today embrace an identity as revolutionaries, but the 2016 presidential campaign of Bernie Sanders tainted the label. Sanders called for dramatic political transformations, and he spoke about the power of economic domination in a way that made sense to poor and working-class Americans, heavily indebted millennials, and those politicized by the Great Recession and Occupy Wall Street. But when he ventured from talk of economic domination to talk of patriarchy and anti-Blackness, his language went flat. His bedrock commitment to American democracy, a political form indelibly colored by settler colonialism, anti-Blackness, patriarchy, and capitalism, made his talk of revolution suspect, even if his rhetoric was necessitated by the context of electoral politics.

While Sanders talked of revolution in terms that would have been familiar to any New Left activist of the 1960s, he seemed ill at ease with the vocabulary native to justice movements of the twenty-first century. For those attentive to the depths of domination, not only along class lines but also along lines of race, gender, sexuality, and disability, revolution was no longer the most comfortable framework. A new framework was emerging that would quickly migrate from one particular organizing context, the U.S. prison system, and come to shape the political imagination of many justice-seeking social movements: abolition.

In less than a decade, mainstream America went from seeing prisons as a solution to seeing them as a problem. A vigorous discussion opened between liberals and leftists about what it would mean to "end mass incarceration." Amid much talk of varying degrees of "reform," prison abolition, once embraced only by a few on the hard left, became a widely held position. If prison is not "correctional" but a continuation of slavery by other means—a claim made plausible by the shackles, forced labor, and disciplinary techniques imposed on a disproportionately Black prison population—then what is needed is to end the system, not to make prisons gentler or reduce their population. Those who proposed a smaller, less harsh slave system were still on the wrong side of history.

In the rapidly moving leftist conversations of the social media era, interest in prison abolition mushroomed. Activists found inspiration in Angela Davis's account of a tradition that situated prison abolition as part of the unfinished work of Reconstruction. For Davis, following W. E. B. Du Bois, the abolitionist movement was as much about building up new social institutions and reweaving the social fabric as about removing the moral abomination of slavery. For racial domination to be excised, legal mechanisms had to be changed, but so did social life. Abolitionists are organizers, gathering communities and catalyzing struggle intended to tear down the old and build up the new. On social media, activists called for abolishing ICE and abolishing the police, and also increasingly identified their political identity as "abolitionist."[5]

In a broad sense, the contours of the abolitionist and revolutionary identities are similar. Both are committed to a radical uprooting of the world order. While that moment of uprooting remains at an unknown distance from the present, it provides the perspective from which to judge present actions: do they bring the revolution, or the abolition of abominable institutions and practices, closer? Both abolitionists and revolutionaries stand in opposition to progressives and reformers, who advocate incremental or discrete responses to social problems. The history of prison reform efforts shows how nearly every purported fix to the criminal justice system has only resulted in more people held in cages. Even supposedly high-tech solutions like electronic monitoring only update the carceral regime, rooted in and driven by capitalism, anti-Blackness, and American delusions of innocence. They do not dismantle it.[6]

Recent abolitionists tend to be more austere than revolutionaries in their descriptions of what is to be purged and what is to come next. In a brief manifesto, for example, the philosopher Lisa Guenther names abolitionism's targets as "oppressive structures," its positive program "imagining, creating, and sustaining the sort of relationships, practices, and institutions that would make oppressive structures obsolete." But talk of oppression, or of oppressive structures, leaves ambiguity that the term *domination* removes. Domination necessarily follows from the paradigm of slavery; oppression suggests any kind of intentionally inflicted suffering. While Black youths increasingly identify as abolitionists, there is also worry that the term is used expansively, moving away from its historical and conceptually necessary focus on Black life and Black dignity. For Guenther, abolitionism looks like "an eschatological opening to the otherwise in the midst of the everyday," an opening that animates social movements. But her expansiveness decenters Black life: social movements come in many forms, some oriented against domination and some not. It is essential to distinguish one kind from the other, and this requires a clear understanding of what the struggle against domination looks like.[7]

In the wake of Donald Trump's 2016 election, an old slogan went viral: "Don't mourn, organize!" The legendary American labor leader Joe Hill supposedly said it to his followers shortly before he was executed in 1915. In its recent usage, the slogan was meant to redeploy those emotionally invested in electoral politics to advance progressive causes by building power at the local level. Community organizing had a surprising career in the national spotlight eight years earlier when Barack Obama was ridiculed by right-wing media for his background as an organizer, even as the methods he imported into electoral politics aided his rise to the presidency. In both cases, *organizing* remains an ambiguous term. It has a long history in the labor movement, another history in the community organizing efforts that descended from Saul Alinsky's work, and still another history as a revolutionary socialist practice. Today, organizing is also entangled with electoral politics at the national and local levels, and it has become professionalized in national networks and training programs. But in its essence, organizing is the paradigm of struggle against domination. Through organizing, in organizing, we achieve dignity.

Like Lynice Pinkard, the Bay Area–based revolutionary socialist group Advance the Struggle also reacted strongly to the 2009 shooting death of Oscar Grant, but it offered quite a different assessment from Pinkard's emphasis on internal struggle for freedom. The group saw the protests against police violence in Oakland as a potentially revolutionary moment that failed to catch on because of failures in organizing. The protests began spontaneously as working-class Black youths took to the streets and were joined by anarchists and cadre from the Revolutionary Communist Party (RCP). Quickly, a group of local nonprofits formed the Coalition against Police Execution. This group attempted to moderate the protests by discouraging looting, fires, and physical confrontation, and to direct the movement toward achieving deliverable goals such as the arrest of Grant's killer and increased police sensitivity training (proposed as a form of "systemic change"). On the other extreme, the RCP positioned itself as leading a radical alternative response and called for high school students to strike. The strike it organized attracted only a few dozen students, along with a graying RCP cadre. The group took to the street, blocking traffic, and its members were violently attacked and arrested by Oakland police—the older, predominantly white RCP cadre having taken themselves out of harm's way when the police moved in. In short, the forms of "organizing" offered by the nonprofit sector and by old-fashioned revolutionary socialists both failed to adequately respond to the political moment.[8]

Before the RCP-led high school walkout, Oakland high school students had been organizing their own walkout without any direction from their elders. But that walkout was called off when the student leaders found themselves incarcerated: they were arrested at the RCP protest. In Advance the Struggle's assessment, "It would have been possible to organize a major unpermitted protest of many thousands of Oakland residents to march through working class neighborhoods." These protests could have been structured so as to invite new participants, educate the masses, and accelerate future organizing and action around police violence and other forms of domination. This did not happen because no infrastructure was in place to support the organizing efforts of those most affected by domination—for example, the Oakland students attempting to organize their own walkout. Since the end of the Oakland-based Black Panther Party, organizing in the Bay Area had splintered among the powerful, liberal-aligned nonprofit sector; a few tiny, insular, sclerotic revolutionary socialist groups like RCP; and activists who showed up at a protest now and then but were not embedded in structures to orient and sustain organizing. Advance the Struggle called for an end to dogmatism and careerism, and for building organizations rooted in Black, working-class communities that are continually refining their analysis of domination and their tactics of struggle.[9]

Advance the Struggle was among a handful of new revolutionary socialist groups formed in the twenty-first-century United States, often with many millennial members, that sought to give revolution a more concrete shape than the buzzy abolitionists but also sought to avoid the dogmatism that characterized many late twentieth-century Marxist groups. These groups shared a commitment to challenging systems of domination beyond capitalism, and to demonstrating how capitalism, racism, patriarchy, homophobia, and domination interlock. They were ambivalent toward unions, suspicious of the professionalization of union organizing and the development of labor bureaucracy, but appreciative of unions' role in struggle and hopeful that new forms of labor organizing could invigorate the revolutionary struggle. Finally and crucially, they shared a commitment to the self-emancipation of those who face domination. Party elites, nonprofit professionals, and casual activists will not bring revolution; they are engaged in simulacra of organizing that reinforce the status quo. Those who have endured domination are formed by struggle, gaining the experiences and skills necessary for a life of self-determination. A revolutionary organization has a vital role in catalyzing, but not leading, this organizing. It incubates struggle, providing a forum for reflection on members' involvement in particular organizing projects, allows members to educate themselves on the history and current state of struggle beyond their immediate context, and offers theoretical frameworks that connect particular struggles with the overarching revolutionary struggle.[10]

The Haitian revolution is the paradigm: slaves organizing themselves to overthrow their masters. C. L. R. James, the preeminent analyst of that revolution, has become a particularly inspirational theorist. A Black Trinidadian, James studied revolutionary theory and the history of struggle while living in the Caribbean, the United Kingdom, and the United States. For a few years in the late 1940s and 1950s, he, Raya Dunayevskaya, a Russian-born Jew, and Grace Lee, a Chinese American, led the Johnson-Forest Tendency, named after the pseudonyms of James and Dunayevskaya, a revolutionary socialist group whose views foreshadowed (and often influenced) those of recent revolutionary organizations. Working intensely together first in New York and then in Detroit, the Johnson-Forest leaders developed a sophisticated theoretical framework to motivate their focus on the self-organization of the working class, particularly among Black communities. Party elites and charity workers were excluded from their vision: the Johnson-Forest Tendency believed that the authorities on liberation were those experiencing domination most intensely. To put this view into practice, the group created a newspaper whose main content consisted of letters from Black and working-class readers; revolutionary intellectuals were tasked with commenting on these texts, offering historical and international comparisons, and explicating the insights they held for clarifying the struggle.[11]

The Hungarian revolution in 1956 demonstrated the promise of this approach, and the Johnson-Forest position was most fully developed in the three leaders' analysis of this event. They had always been suspicious of both capitalism and state socialism. Both promised freedom but actually concentrated power in the hands of elites, ignoring the masses' ability to govern themselves. In Hungary, the masses were pushing away the labor bureaucrats and the Soviets, who were engaged in economic domination. The revolution started on the shop floor, when workers' councils took over the management of factories. According to James and his collaborators, "The secret of the Workers Councils" was that "they do not have to exercise any domination over people." They could attend to the particularities of their situation: the abilities of different workers, what needed to be produced, and the processes of production. Previously, professional managers had dominated, treating workers and products as abstractions, and in their attempts to maximize efficiency they acted arbitrarily on the workers they oversaw, actually decreasing efficiency.[12]

As the Johnson-Forest leaders saw it, the revolutionary actions in Hungary happened more or less simultaneously and spontaneously across the nation. This proved their idea that leadership by a vanguard of revolutionary elites is unnecessary; the working class understands, better than anyone else, the domination it faces and how to respond. Workers' councils not only fought for and gained control of factories, they also created political discussion groups to deliberate on their local and national struggles. In a factory, co-workers find ways to look out for each other and to undermine those who would dominate them. The Johnson-Forest leaders pointed to a U.S. factory where a worker became disabled and his fellow workers, defying management, arranged for his duties to be redistributed so that he could keep his job. In general, those living under domination find ways to enforce collective discipline, ensuring cooperation directed at their shared aims without punitive structures.[13]

All over the world, the lives of those who endure domination are partially but never fully shaped by it. As the Johnson-Forest leaders put it, "The working class in every country lives its own life, makes its own experiences, seeking always to create forms and realize values which may originate directly from its organic opposition to official society, but are shaped by its experiences in cooperative labor." Put another way, two sources blend in the culture of those enduring domination: struggle against domination and collective life and work, each sharpening the other. Even if there is not yet revolutionary activity or organization, not yet workers' councils or their analogues, there is fertile ground for revolution in the cultures of factory workers, poor Black folks, women working as domestics, and any other group enduring domination. These cultures are inevitably derided by the middle class; they fundamentally threaten its way of existence, for each of these cultures contains a foretaste of the socialist world, the world free of domination. They brim with energy and creativity, still evident despite the efforts of the forces of domination to delegitimize and suppress them.[14]

Instead of imposing a vision of how freedom is to be achieved, or of leadership in the struggle, for the Johnson-Forest leaders "the first duty of the organization is to place at the disposal of the working class [read: groups experiencing domination] all possible means, material and intellectual, of expressing itself, its own conditions of life, and its own aims." Organizers, through the discipline provided by membership in a group like Johnson-Forest, are to function as catalysts, spotlighting and accelerating the struggle against domination already in progress. Each site where domination is experienced (in the Marxist tradition, each factory) is isolated from every other, physically and socially—partly because those who benefit from systems of domination try to preserve them. If only those at each site of domination could know that they did not struggle alone, that others were struggling against related forces of domination just down the street and around the world: sharing this information is one of the tasks of organizers. Their second task is to cut through domination's obfuscation about itself. The master makes it look like he is from a chosen race, that he has always been in charge, that science requires him to be in charge. Organizers demystify the powerful and name the structures of domination that guarantee their power—structures that may be unknown to the powerful themselves. These two facets of organizers' work, of revolutionaries' work, complement each other. The more domination is demystified, the clearer it becomes how to best amplify the voices of those struggling at the local level, whose struggles are suppressed by domination. As local struggles are amplified, the contours and machinations of domination become increasingly clear.[15]

The third and final task of organizers in the Johnson-Forest tradition is to clarify the theory of struggle. This can only happen collectively, in an organization, and that organization must consist of a mix of those on the front lines of domination and intellectuals devoted to studying it. Such a mixture is the best that can be done, structurally, to respond to the fact that there will always be those who purport to offer a theory of struggle and attract followers among those who struggle, but whose theory is contaminated by elements of domination. Advance the Struggle's analysis of the Oscar Grant fallout explores this phenomenon, showing how the nonprofit sector and certain supposedly revolutionary organizations offer theories of struggle contaminated by economic or racial domination. When organizers rely on theories that have fixed, positive content, they become dogmatic and attend only to those struggles that are articulated in just the right way—where the criteria for correctness are set by the forces they struggle against. As the Johnson-Forest leaders write, "It is as if a drowning man with the water already in his mouth demanded a certificate of navigation before allowing a boat's crew to save him."[16]

The other sort of positive content to be wary of, closely related to criteria for the shape of struggle, is in the vision of what the world without domination will look like. Organizers can amplify the imaginative work that naturally happens in local struggles regarding what life will look like when their goals are achieved. But they ought to consider such imaginings in a separate register from the theory of domination, which must remain austere and uncontaminated by particularities grown of local contexts that, in a world full of domination, would taint the theory itself. Rather, organizers believe that those enduring domination most intensely have the capacity and vision to shape a future world where there are no kings, bosses, or prison guards.[17]

C. L. R. James was a great revolutionary theorist who helped lead important experiments in the practice of organizing, but his life was rather tragic. At its end, he was living alone in a tiny flat in the London neighborhood of Brixton, reading books and then, when his eyes began to fail, watching television. A white woman who had recently finished her undergraduate degree at Cambridge came upon him and, bedazzled, moved in across the street, spending hours listening to him talk and supposedly collaborating on his autobiography, a project that would never approach completion. James had been married and divorced three times and felt, in retrospect, that he had behaved badly each time. He could only find pleasure in dominating women, he neglected them, and he was unable to communicate his emotions. He and his colleagues lauded those enduring domination for being able to "say precisely what they want and when," but when his second wife, Constance Webb, said to him, "Tell me what you want from me, what you want me to do," James remained mute, uncomprehending. His own life was contaminated by domination, by patriarchal habits and ideas, even as he helped inspire a struggle to cleanse the world of such habits.[18]

More than just illustrating the personal and organizational pathologies that accompany charismatic leadership, James's life reveals the tragic situation in which Black intellectuals find themselves. Revolutionary potential rests with those struggling on the ground against domination, those on the metaphorical shop floor. In James's view, intellectuals work alongside those on the front lines of struggle to offer conceptual and material resources, connect struggles, unmask the forces of domination, and clarify theory, but intellectuals are structurally compromised. To become intellectuals they had to be formed in the world of those who dominate, in the house of the master, and no amount of struggle can fully purge that formation. James was educated in British colonial schools, he learned to love language by reading Thackeray's *Vanity Fair* over and over, and he described himself throughout his life as a "puritan." In contrast, those who grew up fully under the thumb of domination certainly internalize ideas and habits of domination, but these are held loosely and are readily stripped away through collective struggle, even if, short of the eschaton, the revolution itself, some ideas and habits of domination remain. In short, James and those like him, myself included, are blocked from fully realizing Black dignity.[19]

When the revolution comes, revolutionaries and organizers will no longer be necessary; their organizational structures will dissolve as those who have endured domination, whose capacity for self-determination has been honed through struggle, are now able to govern themselves. On the Johnson-Forest model, the likelihood that intellectuals will have a role to play in that world seems negligible; their chances of surviving the revolution are like the rich man's chances of going to heaven. This is not a reason for intellectuals to withdraw from revolutionary activity, only for them to recognize the tragedy of their situation. By definition, intellectuals are suspicious of the wisdom of the world, of the ruses of domination, and cannot rest comfortably in illusion. If they are honest, which is to say if they are truly intellectuals, they will organize together with those most affected by domination, even if their own cause is likely hopeless. Examining domination in laboratory conditions, the Black intellectual is neither master nor slave. Rather, she is a sympathizer and propagandist who takes her lead from the struggles of those enslaved but whose lifestyle depends on the comfort provided by slave labor. When those enslaved succeed in their struggle against their masters, the sympathizer no longer has a role and appears deeply compromised. In Haiti after the revolution, the middle-class sympathizers who escaped with their lives no longer had a home on the island.

With the institutionalization of Black studies and the professionalization of the Black intellectual, even graver pathologies attach to that role. At worst, the professional Black intellectual is not a friend of the slave but a slave catcher. She is tasked with explaining the world of Blacks and our struggles to a largely white audience. She develops tools, methods, and discipline for the task and is accountable to predominantly white institutions (university administrators, magazine editors, television producers). To be credible to her audience, she must identify herself with the struggle, presenting herself as part caricature of the Black masses, part sage—quoting Tupac and Beyoncé, John Dewey and Michel Foucault. Slave catchers come in several varieties: systematic and thorough (social scientists), those who seduce with apparent sympathy (humanists), and those who are straightforwardly evil. Recently, another species has appeared: those who pose as runaways, embracing the language of fugitivity while capturing with concepts (*fugitive* concepts!) the political and aesthetic performances of the fugitive for display at Negrophilic academic presses and conferences. To be clear, the problem is not that contemporary intellectuals are writing about Black people. It is that they produce scholarship on Black people that is antiquarian or monumental, that is not oriented by struggle or accountable to those who struggle.[20]

In an essay titled "Black Study, Black Struggle," the historian Robin Kelley reflects on the ambivalence of Black intellectuals. For them, the university can be a site of contest where knowledge is produced and organized in a way that reproduces racial domination. It can also be a site of struggle, as the Black student uprisings under the sign of Black Lives Matter made clear. At the same time, universities clearly function to reproduce systems of economic and racial domination. Protesters often call for them to provide more resources for Black students and Black scholarship, but the effect is inevitably to grow rather than shrink the mechanisms of domination. In response to this apparent trap, Kelley points to the origins of Black studies as a field attached to grassroots Black social movements, deeply engaged with organic intellectuals, and accountable to communities struggling against domination. While the professionalization of the field has made a full return to those origins impossible, Kelley proposes an effort to recover some of the early spirit of Black studies by encouraging informal study groups that operate at universities' edges.[21]

Unspoken but felt in Kelley's analysis is Black intellectuals' continuing attachment to the university as a privileged site of struggle. Yet it is simply a quirk that certain vocations are housed in and supported by universities while others are not. Hundreds of thousands, maybe millions of Americans consider themselves poets and guitar players, but the American academy provides only a handful of jobs for poets, and even fewer for guitar players. In contrast, the vocation of the amateur philosopher, historian, or social theorist is the realm of a handful of eccentrics; universities employ tens of thousands of people under these titles (though the actual content of their jobs often consists primarily of teaching these activities rather than doing them). In other words, because of the contingent fact that universities employ a large number of people with job titles like "philosopher," "historian," and "social theorist," it seems natural to look to universities, or their margins, as the home of Black intellectual work and struggle. This stance is often accompanied by a thinly disguised narrative of racial uplift and respectability, celebrating the achievements of Black youths accepted to college, becoming valedictorians, gaining honorifics, being granted tenure, and entering university management. At the same time that racial domination is challenged, social and economic domination (of which academic status is emblematic) is reinforced. While contemporary activist culture has started to name and challenge carceral feminism—the attempt to challenge male domination by calling for more carceral domination, for sexual offenders to receive ever-longer prison sentences as well as more generally embracing punitive responses to harm—there is not yet a discourse that names and challenges the glorification of Black academic "achievements."

Following Lynice Pinkard and Huey P. Newton, what is needed for those who embrace Black struggle is revolutionary suicide. They must examine their impulses toward security and respectability and purge their attachments to the institutions and practices that feed those impulses. Being near universities offers some Blacks comfort, even as they rage against universities' anti-Blackness. Such attachments must be suppressed for struggle to be rightly oriented against domination. It may very well be that the university is one among many important sites of struggle, and the availability of students exploring new ideas and primed for action by absurd debt loads and racially toxic cultures makes fertile ground for organizing. But the historic over-privileging of universities as sites of struggle calls for a compensatory de-privileging, an investment in developing intellectual cultures and networks struggling against domination entirely disconnected from the work life of those involved.[22]

Philosophy begins with domination: Plato imagines humanity shackled. He depicts the philosopher as a heroic man, loosed from his chains, who comes to know the true form of reality beyond the cave where he and his fellows were bound. When he returns to the cave, his ideas are dismissed as unbelievable; the other prisoners want to stay where they are. For Nietzsche, philosophy also begins with domination: those who live under the arbitrary power of strong nobles organize themselves, catalyzed by the intellectual work of religious leaders, to transform the world. Those who were previously enslaved come to dominate, their power naturalized by their manipulation of language (redefining "good" and "evil") and by their intellectual work making the way things are now, with them in charge, seem as if it has always been so and always will be. (Nietzsche is not happy with this transformation: in his view, the experience of domination contaminates the new regime of meaning created by the formerly enslaved.)[23]

For both Plato and Nietzsche, the slave transforms the world by overthrowing domination: through conceptual clarity in Plato's case, and through conceptual innovation and organizing in Nietzsche's. In both cases, the transformation is the result of personal experience.

Plato's slave-philosopher sees the light himself and gradually achieves clarity; Nietzsche's slave-philosophers (or slave-priests) are "cellar rats full of revenge and hatred" motivated by *ressentiment*. Neither inherits a tradition of slave-philosophy to which the individual slave-philosopher can be held accountable. Indeed, this seems impossible: if the slave were part of a tradition, he would not be enslaved. In laboratory conditions—as in the Middle Passage—history and community are stripped from the enslaved. It is only from that position that the slave-philosophers' radical innovations, so disconnected from the worlds in which they develop, seem possible.[24]

But the Black tradition is unlike any other. It is a revolutionary tradition that does not take as its subject those with dark skin, those with African genes, or those called "African American" by people around them. The Black tradition names as its subject those who face the domination of slavery and its afterlives, the purest form of domination we find in the world. The Black tradition includes those who experienced the Middle Passage, those who lived enslaved in the Americas, those who lived under post-slavery regimes of domination in the Americas, and those who face the master's force today because of their perceived association with the enslaved, including Black folks in prisons, in cars, in welfare offices and corporate offices, and even in political office.

Because the Black tradition is held together by the experience of enduring and struggling against domination, it takes a different shape from other traditions. National, ethnic, and religious traditions purport to name people and their history bound together by shared practices and, implicit in those practices, shared values. The constitution of such traditions is always infected by domination. Systems of domination determine who counts as an exemplary figure in the tradition and whose voices and values are erased. Traditions infected with domination themselves dominate: they impose the will of another arbitrarily on those whom the tradition claims. An American, for example, as a participant in the American tradition, ought to follow the norms and values of her supposed forefathers, white and wealthy men; otherwise, she will face reprimand or alienation. Certainly traditions can be contested and redefined—this is part of the work of struggle against domination—but inevitably they remain entangled with domination.

Except the Black tradition. The norms of Blackness, of those enslaved and those facing slavery's aftereffects, are oriented by one value: the end of domination. To be initiated into this tradition is to join the struggle—the struggle that brings with it dignity. To join the Black tradition is not to subject oneself to a new form of domination because the content of the Black tradition is the struggle against domination. The content of the tradition allows us to realize our most deeply human desire, to attend to who we are beyond what the world says we are, beyond the objects that domination would make us into.

Just as the primal scene of master and slave leans on ideal types not found in the actual, messy world, labeling the tradition of Blackness as being essentially about struggle also invokes ideal types. But traditions, by their very nature, lean on ideal types (the ideal American, the ideal Jew, the ideal Indian American), so it is not a problem that the Black tradition does so as well. Forces of domination distort our perception of the Black tradition, turning its essential value away from the struggle against domination by focusing on social practices attached to specific elements of culture, specific geographical locations, or certain types of Black folks (for example, the respectable ones). Part of the struggle against domination is the struggle to properly recognize, articulate, and participate in the Black tradition, and to avoid counterfeits—a never-ending site of contestation. Certain genres of storytelling tend to misrepresent the Black tradition: histories of great men fall into this category, but also chronological accounts, with their implied assumptions about transmission of authority, as well as synchronic accounts of

Black culture that convey a sense of domination's fixity. Articulating the Black tradition faithfully as a revolutionary tradition requires moving back and forth through time to demonstrate the continuity among forms of struggle without presuming descent; and it requires thwarting monumental and antiquarian tendencies by starting with and remaining accountable to the shape of the struggle today, in the storyteller's world and life.[25]

There is an upsurge in rigorous philosophy of race being written today, but this is not Black philosophy. Nor is the imaginative work theorizing Blackness as fugitivity, celebrating the way Blackness is found dancing otherwise in the interstices of institutions of domination. There is a widening landscape of scholarship studying Black culture; this is also not Black philosophy. There is much being written by activists reflecting on their experience in the struggle; this is still not philosophy. As Black studies scholar Sylvia Wynter points out, the feminist movement in the 1960s developed a sharp analysis of patriarchy, but the Black freedom movement never developed a corresponding analysis of racial domination, focusing instead on naming empirical forms of oppression and celebrating Black resilience. In recent years, Black youths immersed in collective struggle have led the way in beginning to thematize anti-Blackness as a system of domination, and as the paradigm for domination itself. Faithful to the Black tradition, performing Black dignity, they are moving back and forth between historical resources, forms of aesthetic performance and imagination, and on-the-ground protest. Doing so makes visible the ontological difference of domination: Black philosophy begins.[26]

AFTERWORD

How to Live with Dignity

How ought one to live, given the realities of domination? Most of the time, the world provides reasons for action, including moral action, at an ontic level. Social practices and the values implicit in their histories authorize and direct how we live. If we want to be good in the ontic sense, we perform the practices our culture considers good. To be excellent is to model one's life on the life of a person acclaimed as excellent. The struggle against domination provides reasons for action whose provenance is in the ontological register; these can trump ontic reasons for action. Struggle gives us reason to do things that the world says we ought not to do, and it defeats the world's reasons. Unfortunately, we never have direct access to the ontological register. We are always struggling to discern the shape of domination and to orient struggle rightly. If we had perfect access to the ontological register, the reasons for action emanating from that register would always defeat the reasons of the ontic register, but as it is, only when our clarity about the ontological register passes a certain threshold do its reasons win the day.[1]

Given our poor access to the ontological register, to knowledge about domination, we can employ certain heuristics—ascetic practices—to avoid running afoul of the struggle against domination and to improve our epistemic access to that register. These also offer preemptive reasons for action. Practices that closely resemble the generic primal scene of domination are always to be avoided as a moral absolute. You should never own a slave, rape another person, or steal land from an indigenous person. Anyone who engages in these practices, regardless of their cultural context, deserves condemnation. Other principles may be slightly more controversial: you should never work as a prison guard, for example, or purchase land that was recently appropriated from its inhabitants. A second heuristic: you should avoid comfortably inhabiting identities that are closely associated with domination. Those identities are recognizable from the set of practices they involve, practices that function as a cluster to perform identity even as they are each individually innocuous (for race: living in certain neighborhoods, shopping at certain stores, wearing certain clothes, speaking in certain styles; for gender: having certain mannerisms and habits of speech, having a certain level of involvement in housework and childrearing, or wearing certain sorts of clothes). Many of the practices in the clusters associated with whiteness, masculinity, wealth, Americanness, and so on should be avoided.[2]

Other moral heuristics limit our affective investment in the norms of our culture and so open us to responding rightly when we cross a threshold of certainty about the struggle against domination. For example, asceticism, the habitual abstention from certain cultural practices—such as fasting regularly from food or the internet—reminds us that we should not act like the world has the last word. Similarly, radically asymmetric relational practices, where we give a huge amount and receive little in return, remind us that the world's calculus, where relationships are considered just if they balance out, is itself implicated in the logic of domination. The biblical parable of the workers in the vineyard, who each labor different numbers of hours but all receive the same pay, illustrates that heavenly calculus is unintelligible from a worldly perspective. Romantic relationships often offer lessons in relating in ways that do not add up rationally. Their very imbalance can be what makes them fulfilling.

While retaining a certain distance from the culture in which one lives is necessary for remaining open to struggle as it bubbles up from the ontological depths, this distance should not be confused with a thoroughgoing counter-cultural attitude. Remaining open to struggle requires a minimum level of affective investment in one's culture, for the struggle against domination involves a mixture of the ontological and the ontic. The primal scene of domination exists in the ontological register, but the manifestations of domination and the optimal shape of struggle are in the ontic register. Discerning those ontic dimensions requires fluency in and concern for one's own culture.

Culture provides language, concepts, and repertoires for action, feeling, and thought. To judge our reasons as reasonable and our feelings as apt, we must look to our culture for criteria. But culture, being infected by systems of domination, does not have the last word. Appreciating this opens an ontological register that also motivates reasons and feelings. When we struggle against domination, that struggle is motivated by the ontological register; the reasons for action in struggle and the feelings elicited by struggle are judged according to the ontological register and may seem irrational and inapt according to the criteria employed in the ontic register. Love and rage, for example, have different meanings in any given cultural context and as they relate to the struggle against domination. So does dignity. But struggle happens in the real world, in a particular context, employing ontic raw material. Once we attend to domination in the ontological register, we are able to interpret an element of culture as having one meaning in the ontic register (participating in a particular social practice) and another meaning in the ontological register, as oriented toward or against the struggle against domination. In short, we have to be able to cut through a jumble of culture that captures our attention in order to notice the workings of domination and the struggle against domination. But once we do, we are able to access a realm of truth that transcends culture. With struggle comes a kind of flourishing that we can never achieve simply by inhabiting a culture well.

Systems of domination partially constitute our worlds and all objects in them, including ourselves. The ways we think, feel, act, and imagine are all partially shaped by a given system of domination, for example, anti-Blackness. We are formed by our parents, our teachers, our neighbors, police officers, and colleagues into creatures who inhabit the world's norms. For French philosopher Louis Althusser, these systems of norms, ideology, are calcified. As we are formed into the world, we are formed into ideology, which seems natural but actually serves the interests of the ruling class. According to Althusser, we once focused primarily on the power of the state, the paradigm of which is the king's ability to arbitrarily impose his will on the masses. Today, however, all sorts of social institutions—educational, religious, entertainment, and cultural—do the work of the state, arbitrarily imposing a will, now not of the king but of the ruling class.[3]

Althusser's depiction of the world is suffocating. While he promises to pluralize the sites of struggle against the ruling class, so that seizing state power is no longer the only goal of struggle, his framework presents each of us as fully formed by ruling-class interests. When we treat domination as an ontological problem, by contrast, there is not a stiff line connecting ruling-class ideas and the formation of subjects in the world. Rather, there are multiple systems of domination, each contributing to the formation of subjects. A human being is never simply the sum of the contributions of all systems of domination. There is always a remainder.

This remainder cannot be named, for it could only be named in a language infected by domination. The human casts a shadow on the ontological register. The evidence in the ontic register for this irreducible aspect of the human is the friction we see in systems of domination. Anti-Blackness does not work perfectly; occasionally, the white police officer doubts himself. Those humans whom economic domination would turn into machinery call in sick, pilfer products, or drop a wrench into the equipment—or perform acts of altruism at the workplace. From the perspective of domination, these are inefficiencies to be corrected. In fact they are reminders that the human is primed for struggle, for dignity. When the points of friction in a system of domination become aware of each other, talk to each other about a system of domination that affects them, and plan collective action against it, then we realize our humanity. Our ontic and ontological forms come into alignment. The Black studies theorist Sylvia Wynter calls on us to recognize the way the category of Man was constituted by racial, colonial, and patriarchal forms of domination, and to search for the concrete human lurking beneath the abstract category. Wynter is right, helpfully filling in the particular character of domination in the West and tracing how systems of domination interlock, but she underemphasizes the positive side of the story: where we find collective struggle against domination, we find what is human. Black dignity is human dignity.[4]

In addition to naturalizing themselves, systems of domination work very hard to conceal that the human has more than an ontic existence. This knowledge, should it spread, poses an existential threat to a system of domination. The very essence of domination, revealed in its primal scene, is to treat a human as less than human, as animal-like or machine-like. When we witness such treatment, our emotional response rises from an ontological level: we feel moral horror. This feeling tracks abominations, the label we give when the human in another is grotesquely being ignored. It is what we feel when we see children locked in cages, state executions, or a battered woman's face. The stakes are high when it comes to moral horror: systems of domination work very hard to mask, redirect, or otherwise confuse our perception of it, for when moral horror is rightly perceived, it acts as an accelerant to struggles against domination.

For some time, it has been fashionable for cultural studies scholars, particularly queer theorists, to condemn normativity as such. The thought was that if Althusser is right and social norms interlock, all advancing and concealing the interests of the ruling class, every site where a norm is contested is praiseworthy because it marks a threat to ruling-class power. The more norms you contest in the way you live your life, the bigger the threat, culminating in queerness as an ideal type, meaning both those whose lifestyles contest social norms around sexuality and those who live in ways that contest all norms. When we accept the stickiness of social norms to each other but focus on their relationship to multiple systems of domination instead of positing that they directly express the will of a single, coherent ruling class, it is no longer praiseworthy simply to contest any randomly chosen norm. Rather, we must discern the precise shape of a system of domination, following from its primal scene, and use that knowledge as a starting point for deciding on the best tactics for struggle against that particular system. Note that this is not pragmatism: domination exists on an ontological level, and it is only through thinking the ontological and the ontic together that struggle can be properly oriented.[5]

Is there such a thing as ontological virtue, virtue that participates in flourishing through struggle? Virtue usually refers to moral dispositions that a culture finds praiseworthy, and that, when practiced together, lead to a flourishing life. Philosopher Lisa Tessman argues that certain virtues are "burdened": we need them in order to survive or contest oppression, but they do not lead to flourishing. Practicing them leads to a kind of second-order oppression of already oppressed communities. But these virtues still operate at an ontic level: they are habits cultivated in communities of the oppressed, characteristic of those communities. Because they are habitual, formed in community, and dependent on community for their recognition, virtues are firmly rooted in the ontic level. At the ontic level, we can orient ourselves toward the ontological, toward struggle, only through heuristics. If there is one exception, it is a virtue excluded from the traditional lists, the virtue of attention to self, others, and world. Domination tells a false story, and it contaminates our perception to make that story seem true. But if we attend carefully enough, for long enough, in one particular direction, we may catch glimpses of the way domination's story mismatches its purported objects. What we notice may be negative, something missing that was expected; it may be a moment of paradox. As we attend more, we discern the shape of domination casting a shadow on our world, and we notice points of struggle.[6]

In short, the deepest kind of flourishing we can experience, the flourishing that accompanies struggle, cannot be achieved by following certain moral rules or copying certain moral habits. Such rules and habits can lead to ontic flourishing, which follows from being well acculturated; but the more we taste ontic flourishing, the less we are interested in the ontological. The less we notice the domination that infects our world. Part of the asceticism required for struggle involves resisting the temptation to pursue ontic flourishing, even as we do not tear ourselves fully away from the world. We are aided in this task by struggle itself, as it provides a foretaste of a world without domination. There is nothing more desirable than that. Yet we must also resist the temptation to live entirely oriented around struggle. We do not have sufficient access to the shape of domination to warrant that. The result would inevitably be an attempt to smuggle the ontic into the ontological, and what purports to be struggle against domination will only be counter-cultural practice that remains within the orbit of domination.

The goal of the struggle against domination is, tautologically, the abolition of systems of domination. If certain institutions or practices in the world derive from a primal scene of domination, then those institutions or practices ought to be abolished. But if everything is tainted by systems of domination, doesn't this mean we should abolish everything? Yes. The place to begin is the end of the world. That is a matter of principle, an ontological statement. Back in the world, one of the ways the struggle against domination manifests is through naming discrete targets and calling for their elimination. Contemporary abolitionists are often quite clear on this point: among themselves, they agree that patriarchy needs to be abolished, racism needs to be abolished, capitalism needs to be abolished, settler colonialism needs to be abolished. Speaking in public, they employ a rhetoric that focuses on prisons or Immigration and Customs Enforcement or the police. Acting in public, in protests and community meetings, they advocate policies that shrink rather than inflate the systems they seek to abolish; abolition itself might never be mentioned. If a county jail is overcrowded, abolitionists refuse to support the construction of a new facility, even though this would purportedly be the humane solution. (In reality, jail populations expand to fill capacity.) Political reasoning in this mode starts with the ontological claim, abolish everything, moves to the ontic claim, abolish these particularly egregious institutions of domination, and then moves to the practical, supporting policies that move in the direction of abolishing those institutions. The sequence here is crucial. It differentiates abolitionists from reformers, who would start with policy proposals meant to address a worldly problem and look warily at an idea like prison abolition as, at best, something for the very long term.

Discerning the appropriate tactics for struggle against domination is difficult work, and individually our clarity remains limited. Collectively, however, we are better able to identify systems of domination and better able to discern tactics to extirpate them. While the struggle against domination can happen individually, it achieves a new level of intensity and focus when it is collective. But even collectively, there will be times when we have an intuition that domination is at work and that there ought to be a way to struggle against it, but we do not reach a sufficient level of confidence to act or to speak out. Once we see ourselves participating in struggle, with its promise of freedom from domination not only as an end but in the performance of struggle itself, we are tempted to look for more and more places in the world to struggle, ever lowering the threshold of knowledge about domination we need to act. Soon, we are intervening in worldly matters like electoral politics in the name of struggle, and elevating them to an ontological significance that they do not deserve. One of the challenges of the struggle is to avoid becoming intoxicated by the struggle.

Not all humans have equal access to knowledge about domination and the struggle against it. Those who themselves endure particularly intense forms of domination gain expertise. Domination constitutes our world, but its force is felt unevenly. To those in positions of relative privilege, domination presents as smoothness, comfort, a world where everything makes sense and fits together in an orderly way. This is the world of the master: each element ostensibly in his control. When domination presents in this way, seemingly frictionless, it is difficult to gain critical leverage that would put it in perspective. Turning to history, or to other contexts where domination manifests differently, may be the best option. Then the knowledge of domination is at arm's length. If this observer (white, middle class) immerses himself in the world of those experiencing domination, he may gain some insights, but his judgment remains suspect.

In contrast, for those of us who experience domination with special intensity, it is perfectly obvious that some force is arbitrarily intervening in our lives. The slick stories domination tells that may seduce whites and the middle class fall on deaf ears when they are told to poor Black folks. As much as systems of domination try to convince some people that they are less than human, that they deserve the treatment they receive, and as much as the vulnerable may regurgitate such stories, they are never completely accepted. Furthermore, where domination is most intense, struggle against domination on a small scale is especially plentiful. Mere survival requires familiarity with the tactics of struggle. In short, those who face intense domination have greater epistemic access to domination and to the shape of struggle against it than those who live relatively insulated from its blunt force. The epistemic privilege of the oppressed is defeasible: in a world saturated with domination, everyone's perception is clouded. The greater the number of oppressed people who discern and respond together to domination, the greater the clarity—an order of magnitude greater than the clarity available to those in positions of relative privilege. Importantly, epistemic privilege does not attach to a culture or to an ethnic group. It attaches to individuals and collectives in action, organizing against domination.[7]

The best education in struggle is struggle: in the process of struggle, one begins to learn the tricks domination uses to conceal itself, the shapes it takes in the world, and the tactics of struggle that are most effective. When struggle is collective, shared reflection accelerates learning. What role, then, can philosophy play? Since domination contaminates even our thoughts and reasoning, as well as cultural practices like philosophy, it would seem to be of little use. There might be value in convening those who struggle in different contexts, across place and time, to share notes, but what else can philosophy add?

Even in collective struggle, certain disorienting habits of thought remain deeply entrenched. To connect the many subtle manifestations of domination with a primal scene of domination, resisting the urge to reduce struggle to ontic problem-solving, is extremely difficult work. This is where philosophy may help. At its best, philosophy cleaves the ontic and ontological dimensions of feelings, reasoning, and imagining, making clearer what is oriented toward struggle and what secures the hold of domination. Because of philosophy's own potential contamination by domination, it must maintain its rigor. Philosophy becomes an instrument of domination when its effect is comfort: providing a system of order or reasons, or through some other attempt at exhaustiveness. Similarly, philosophy can promise comfort through escapism, by offering an account of the limits of the world and the openings to another world. Finally, philosophy can sanctify the fallenness of the world, commending pragmatic action while the philosopher wallows in the world's tragic nature. Each of these temptations turns philosophy away from its task of rigorously analyzing the struggle against domination.

When philosophy is rightly oriented, it is intertwined with rhetoric. The task they jointly take on is to narrate the connections between primal scenes of domination and domination manifesting in the world. This requires telling stories in worldly terms, using words and images that will move readers to join the struggle. Domination tells its own stories that conceal and naturalize it. The task of the philosopher-rhetorician is to out-narrate domination. She must tell stories about the primal scene of domination and its continuing effects in the world that are so vivid that the stories domination tells about itself begin to seem implausible. Her stories invite her audience to make judgments, to recognize the ways domination has distorted their lives, and to join the struggle. This task is part of the work of struggle. As such, it is best conducted collectively, in groups where those facing the full force of domination are heavily represented. This is not to say that the whole collective must think and write together; that would compromise the rigor of thought, not to mention efficiency. Rather, philosophy is accountable to projects of collective struggle, checking its insights against the intuitions developed through struggle, and itself learning from those insights.

This is a task at which Frederick Douglass excelled. Connecting his own experience with the primal scene of domination in his narrative, he draws them so close that they almost become one and the same. Douglass strove to out-narrate the stories that were told to justify slavery, calling his audience to turn away from them and instead embrace a story of struggle. He wrote and spoke while embedded in a collective of abolitionists struggling together against slavery. It was a rowdy, factious group; with the stakes so high, tempers flared over questions about the appropriate tactics of struggle and the appropriate analysis of racial domination (for example, was slavery so baked into the U.S. Constitution that a new form of government was needed?). Douglass was accountable to the collective of abolitionists, but he also used his own reason and imagination to participate in struggle with his pen and voice as weapons. When he writes, "A man without force is without the essential dignity of humanity," he is writing not only about the dignity performed in his fight with Covey but also about the dignity performed in his narration of that fight, a story that wields its own force.

Douglass is not just offering lessons about philosophy as a profession. He teaches about philosophy as a way of life. The philosophical life involves collective discernment, storytelling, and commitment. It is not a life reserved only for the few; it is open to all. Indeed, it is required of all. It is the intellectual component of the life of Black dignity, just as forms of ascesis are among the practical components. The two go hand in hand: we must live in a way that opens us to discerning domination, and we must rightly discern and respond to domination when we encounter it.

Notes

Chapter 1. Everything Black

1. Martin Luther King, Jr., Nobel Acceptance Speech, https://www.nobelprize.org/prizes/peace/1964/king/26142-martin-luther-king-jr-acceptance-speech-1964/; Stokely Carmichael, *Stokely Speaks: From Black Power to Pan-Africanism* (Chicago: Chicago Review, 2014), 120; Barack Obama, Nobel Acceptance Speech, https://www.nobelprize.org/prizes/peace/2009/obama/26183-nobel-lecture-2009/; Movement for Black Lives platform: https://m4bl.org/policy-platforms; Alicia Garza, "A Herstory of the #BlackLivesMatter Movement," *Feminist Wire* (October 7, 2014), https://www.thefeministwire.com/2014/10/blacklivesmatter-2; Hebah H. Farrag, "The Role of Spirit in the #BlackLivesMatter Movement," *Religion Dispatches* (June 24, 2015), https://religiondispatches.org/the-role-of-spirit-in-the-blacklivesmatter-movement-a-conversation-with-activist-and-artist-patrisse-cullors/; Opal Tometi, "Black Lives Matter," *Guardian* [Nigeria] (January 5, 2020), https://guardian.ng/life/on-the-cover/opal-tometi-black-lives-matter/. Jeannine Marie DeLombard is writing a history of race and dignity in the United States, and I have benefited from exchanges with her and drafts of her work.

2. *We Charge Genocide: The Historic Petition to the United Nations for Relief from a Crime of the United States Government against the Negro People*, ed. William L. Patterson (New York: International, 1970), xiv; *Paul Robeson Speaks: Writings, Speeches, Interviews, 1918–1974*, ed. Philip Sheldon Foner (New York: Brunner/Mazel, 1978), 143. I expand on this analysis of Robeson in Vincent Lloyd, "The Dignity of Paul Robeson," in *Christianity and Human Rights Reconsidered*, ed. Sarah Shortall and Daniel Steinmetz-Jenkins (Cambridge: Cambridge University Press, 2020), 189–204.

3. Ossie Davis is quoted in *Paul Robeson Speaks*, 23; Shana Redmond, *Everything Man: The Form and Function of Paul Robeson* (Durham, NC: Duke University Press, 2020); Paul Robeson, *Here I Stand* (Boston: Beacon, 1971), 11.

4. Langston Hughes, *The Collected Poems of Langston Hughes*, ed. Arnold Rampersad with David Roessel (New York: Knopf, 1994), 205, 339. Copyright © 1951, 1994 by the Estate of Langston Hughes. Within the United States, used by permission of

Alfred A. Knopf, an imprint of the Knopf Doubleday Publishing Group, a division of Penguin Random House LLC. All rights reserved. Outside the United States, reprinted by permission of Harold Ober Associates.

5. Houria Bouteldja, *Whites, Jews, and Us* (South Pasadena, CA: Semiotext(e), 2016), 126.

6. Frederick Douglass, *Life and Times of Frederick Douglass* (Boston: De Wolfe & Fiske, 1892), 177. For another approach to Douglass and dignity, see Nick Bromell, *The Powers of Dignity: The Black Political Philosophy of Frederick Douglass* (Durham, NC: Duke University Press, 2021).

7. Douglass, *Life and Times of Frederick Douglass*, 173.

8. Douglass, *Life and Times of Frederick Douglass*, 177.

9. Douglass, *Life and Times of Frederick Douglass*. On the theological dimensions of dignity, see Vincent Lloyd, "Human Dignity Is Black Dignity," *Church Life Journal* (June 16, 2020), https://churchlifejournal.nd.edu/articles/human-dignity-is-black-dignity/.

10. Martin Luther King, Jr., *The Papers of Martin Luther King, Jr.* (Berkeley: University of California Press, 1997), 3:432. I have benefited from the work of other scholars thinking along related lines: Neil Roberts, *Freedom as Marronage* (Chicago: University of Chicago Press, 2015); Norman Ajari, *La dignité ou la mort: Éthique et politique de la race* (Paris: La Découverte, 2019); George Ciccariello-Maher, "Decolonizing Dignity," unpublished manuscript.

11. See James C. Scott, *Domination and the Arts of Resistance: Hidden Transcripts* (New Haven, CT: Yale University Press, 1990). Dignity as struggle may be found at sites of abundance as well as of deficit, as recent interest in mutual aid as political organizing practice has underscored. Dean Spade, *Mutual Aid: Building Solidarity during This Crisis (and the Next)* (New York: Verso, 2020).

12. See Phillip Pettit, *Republicanism: A Theory of Freedom and Government* (Oxford: Oxford University Press, 1997).

13. Note the parallel to Carl Schmitt's account of the political sovereign as one who decides (i.e., arbitrarily) on the exception. Schmitt argues that many political systems conceal this aspect of sovereignty, leading to pathologies, and the task of the legal or political theorist is to tell a story connecting a particular political system to that primal scene of sovereignty, the scene of sovereign deciding on the exception. Carl Schmitt, *Political Theology* (Chicago: University of Chicago Press, 2005).

14. Civic republicans treat domination itself this way, as an ontic problem requiring mitigation through institution-building and policy fixes. Pettit, *Republicanism*. See also Mary Nyquist, *Arbitrary Rule: Slavery, Tyranny, and the Power of Life and Death* (Chicago: University of Chicago Press, 2015).

15. Jeremy Waldron, *Dignity, Rank, and Rights* (New York: Oxford University Press, 2012), 32; Matthew S. Weinert, *Making Human: World Order and the Global Governance of Human Dignity* (Ann Arbor: University of Michigan Press, 2015), 58.

16. Would humans without a will to dominate still be humans? Would they be a different sort of creature? These are intriguing questions, but they attempt to bring worldly logic into a space of imagining beyond the world.

17. See, for example, Jodi Melamed, *Represent and Destroy: Rationalizing Violence in the New Racial Capitalism* (Minneapolis: University of Minnesota Press, 2011); Critical Ethnic Studies Collective, *Critical Ethnic Studies: A Reader* (Durham, NC: Duke University Press, 2016).

18. Lynice Pinkard, "Revolutionary Suicide: Risking Everything to Transform Society and Live Fully," *Tikkun* 28, no. 4 (Fall 2013): 38.

19. Alicia Garza, "A Love Note to Our Folks," *n + 1* (January 20, 2015), https://nplusonemag.com/online-only/online-only/a-love-note-to-our-folks/; Jamilah King, "#blacklivesmatter: How Three Friends Turned a Spontaneous Facebook Post into a Global Phenomenon," *California Sunday Magazine* (March 1, 2015), https://stories.californiasunday.com/2015-03-01/black-lives-matter/; Alicia Garza, *The Purpose of Power* (New York: One World, 2020).

20. Movement for Black Lives platform: https://m4bl.org/policy-platforms/; Beyoncé's "Formation": https://www.youtube.com/watch?v=WDZJPJV__bQ; D Smoke's "Black Habits": https://www.youtube.com/watch?v=-BCVf3f5Pgg.

21. Another important stream is analysis of racial capitalism. That style of analysis tends toward the political rather than the moral, and it strikes me as less foundational than Black dignity (where capitalism is considered one mode of domination), but I leave it to others to explore what I agree is a crucially important line of inquiry around race and economics. Thanks to Siddhant Issar for pushing me on this point.

22. While many theorists are sometimes described as Afropessimists, the key texts defining the project are Jared Sexton, *Amalgamation Schemes: Antiblackness and the Critique of Multiracialism* (Minneapolis: University of Minnesota Press, 2008); Frank B. Wilderson, III, *Red, White, and Black: Cinema and the Structure of U.S. Antagonisms* (Durham, NC: Duke University Press, 2010); and Wilderson, *Afropessimism* (New York: Liverlight, 2020).

23. Key texts include Fred Moten, *In the Break: The Aesthetics of the Black Radical Tradition* (Minneapolis: University of Minnesota Press, 2003); Moten, "Blackness and Nothingness (Mysticism in the Flesh)," *South Atlantic Quarterly* 112, no. 4 (2013): 737–80; Stefano Harney and Fred Moten, *The Undercommons: Fugitive Planning*

and Black Study (Wivenhoe, UK: Minor Compositions, 2013); and Barnor Hesse, "Escaping Liberty: Western Hegemony, Black Fugitivity," *Political Theory* 42, no. 3 (2014): 288–313.

24. Friedrich Nietzsche, *Untimely Meditations* (Cambridge: Cambridge University Press, 1997); Stephen Best and Sharon Marcus, "Surface Reading," *Representations* 108, no. 1 (Fall 2009): 1–21; Rita Felski, *The Limits of Critique* (Chicago: University of Chicago Press, 2015).

25. See Linda M. G. Zerilli, *A Democratic Theory of Judgment* (Chicago: University of Chicago Press, 2016).

26. See Martha Biondi, *The Black Revolution on Campus* (Berkeley: University of California Press, 2012).

27. See Roderick A. Ferguson, *The Reorder of Things: The University and Its Pedagogies of Minority Difference* (Minneapolis: University of Minnesota Press, 2012); Eli Meyerhoff, *Beyond Education: Radical Studying for Another World* (Minneapolis: University of Minnesota Press, 2019).

28. For an example of the state of the art in academic philosophy of race, see Joshua Glasgow, Sally Haslanger, Chike Jeffers, and Quayshawn Spencer, *What Is Race? Four Philosophical Views* (New York: Oxford University Press, 2019). On the Middle Passage, compare claims about the philosophical import of the Jewish Holocaust, e.g., Emil L. Fackenheim, "The Holocaust and Philosophy," *Journal of Philosophy* 82, no. 10 (October 1985): 505–14.

29. C. L. R. James and Grace C. Lee, *Facing Reality* (Detroit: Bewick, 1974), 65–66. While James and Lee are credited as authors, the book was written by a larger collective.

30. Emmanuel Levinas, *Totality and Infinity: An Essay on Exteriority* (Pittsburgh: Duquesne University Press, 1969).

Chapter 2. Black Rage

1. https://mslaurynhill.com/post/95329923112/black-rage-sketch. I am grateful to Lauryn Hill for permission to include her lyrics. For a thoughtful discussion of Hill and this song, see La Marr Jurelle Bruce, *How to Go Mad without Losing Your Mind: Madness and Black Radical Creativity* (Durham, NC: Duke University Press, 2021).

2. I elaborate on these ideas in Vincent Lloyd, "Anger: A Secularized Theological Concept," *Political Theology* 22, no. 7 (2021): 584–96, where I also discuss postcolonial critics of anger, including Pankaj Mishra and Arjun Appadurai.

3. Nick Bromell, "Democratic Indignation: Black American Thought and the Politics of Dignity," *Political Theory* 41, no. 2 (2013): 285–311.

4. Martin Luther King, Jr., *Where Do We Go from Here: Chaos or Community?* (Boston: Beacon, 2010), 18, 66, 47; King, *A Testament of Hope: The Essential Writings and Speeches of Martin Luther King, Jr.* (San Francisco: HarperSanFrancisco, 1991), 69.

5. Mychal Denzel Smith, "The Function of Black Rage," *Nation* (April 1, 2014), https://www.thenation.com/article/archive/function-black-rage/.

6. bell hooks, *Killing Rage: Ending Racism* (New York: H. Hold, 1995), 19–20.

7. Ellis Cose, *The End of Anger: A New Generation's Take on Race and Rage* (New York: Ecco, 2011); Obama's speech, "A More Perfect Union," is available at https://www.npr.org/templates/story/story.php?storyId=88478467.

8. Smith, "The Function of Black Rage"; Smith, "The Rebirth of Black Rage," *Nation* (August 13, 2015), https://www.thenation.com/article/archive/the-rebirth-of-black-rage/; Ta-Nehisi Coates, *Between the World and Me* (New York: Spiegel & Grau, 2015).

9. Audre Lorde, *Sister Outsider: Essays and Speeches* (Trumansburg, NY: Crossing, 1984), 124–33.

10. Lorde, *Sister Outsider*, 127.

11. Lorde, *Sister Outsider*, 129, 133.

12. Sara Ahmed, *The Cultural Politics of Emotions* (Edinburgh: Edinburgh University Press, 2014), 176.

13. María Lugones, *Pilgrimages / Peregrinajes: Theorizing Coalition against Multiple Oppressions* (Lanham, MD: Rowman & Littlefield, 2003), 112.

14. Austin Channing Brown, *I'm Still Here: Black Dignity in a World Made for Whiteness* (New York: Convergent Books, 2018).

15. Darnell L. Moore, *No Ashes in the Fire: Coming of Age Black & Free in America* (New York: Nation Books, 2018), 182, 230.

16. Brittney Cooper, *Eloquent Rage: A Black Feminist Discovers Her Superpower* (New York: St. Martin's, 2018).

17. Cooper, *Eloquent Rage*, 4.

18. Brittney C. Cooper, *Beyond Respectability: The Intellectual Thought of Race Women* (Urbana: University of Illinois Press, 2017), 58.

19. Cooper, *Beyond Respectability*, 5.

Chapter 3. Black Love

1. Malcolm X, *Malcolm X Speaks: Selected Speeches and Statements,* ed. George Breitman (New York: Grove, 1965), 177.

2. Elizabeth Day, "#BlackLivesMatter: The Birth of a New Civil Rights Movement," *Guardian* (July 19, 2015), https://www.theguardian.com/world/2015/jul/19/

blacklivesmatter-birth-civil-rights-movement; Opal Tometi, Alicia Garza, and Patrisse Cullors-Brignac, "Celebrating MLK Day: Reclaiming Our Movement Legacy," *HuffPost* (January 18, 2015), https://www.huffpost.com/entry/reclaiming-our-movement-l_b_6498400.

3. BYP100 Membership Handbook (June 1, 2018), https://byp100.ourpowerbase.net/sites/default/files/civicrm/persist/contribute/files/2018%20Membership%20Handbook%20.pdf; Charlene A. Carruthers, *Unapologetic: A Black, Queer, and Feminist Mandate for Our Movement* (Boston: Beacon, 2018), 100; Dante Barry, "We Fight, We Love: A Revolutionary Act," *Ebony* (February 11, 2016), https://www.ebony.com/news/we-fight-we-love/.

4. I elaborate on these points about King in Vincent Lloyd, "What Love Is Not: Lessons from Martin Luther King, Jr.," *Modern Theology* 36, no. 1 (2020): 107–20.

5. Martin Luther King, Jr., *The Papers of Martin Luther King, Jr.* (Berkeley: University of California Press, 1992), 2:254, 6:130–31.

6. King, *Papers*, 6:270, 2:442, 3:73.

7. King, *Papers*, 7:507.

8. Martin Luther King, Jr., *A Testament of Hope: The Essential Writings and Speeches of Martin Luther King, Jr.* (San Francisco: HarperSanFrancisco, 1991), 26; King, *Papers*, 6:240.

9. Ralph Ellison, *Invisible Man* (New York: Vintage, 1995), 16.

10. Patrisse Cullors and Robert Ross, "The Spiritual Work of Black Lives Matter," *On Being* (February 18, 2016), https://onbeing.org/programs/patrisse-cullors-and-robert-ross-the-spiritual-work-of-black-lives-matter-may2017/.

11. See Jodi Dean, *Comrade: An Essay on Political Belonging* (New York: Verso, 2019).

12. I elaborate on these accounts of love in Vincent Lloyd, "Eldridge Cleaver, George Jackson, and the Ethics of Love," in *Anti-Blackness and Christian Ethics*, ed. Vincent Lloyd and Andrew Prevot (Maryknoll, NY: Orbis, 2017), 131–49.

13. Eldridge Cleaver, *Soul on Ice* (New York: Dell, 1968), 23.

14. Cleaver, *Soul on Ice*, 19, 149, 18.

15. George Jackson, *Soledad Brother: The Prison Letters of George Jackson* (Chicago: Lawrence Hill Books, 1994), 40.

16. Cleaver, *Soul on Ice*, 19, 27.

17. Jackson, *Soledad Brother*, 112, 76.

18. Jackson, *Soledad Brother*, 122, 227.

19. Cleaver, *Soul on Ice*, 32.

20. Alice Walker, *The Color Purple* (Orlando: Harcourt, 1992), xi, 110, 111; Walker, *In Search of Our Mothers' Gardens: Womanist Prose* (San Diego: Harcourt Brace Jova-

novich, 1983), xi–xii. I suspect this supersessionist view of love overturning all law is not unconnected to Walker's anti-Semitism, a point I develop in Vincent Lloyd, "Love, Judgment, and Anti-Semitism: The Case of Alice Walker," in *The King Is in the Field: Essays in Modern Jewish Politics,* ed. Sam Brody and Julie Cooper (Philadelphia: University of Pennsylvania Press, forthcoming).

21. Lorde writes of the erotic, but the erotic is often received by her readers as love, and I refer to it as love here. Audre Lorde, *Sister Outsider: Essays and Speeches* (Trumansburg, NY: Crossing, 1984), 53–59.

22. Assata Shakur, *Assata: An Autobiography* (Westport, CT: Lawrence Hill Books, 1987); Audre Lorde, "For Assata," in *Black Unicorn: Poems* (New York: Norton, 1995), 28.

23. Shakur, *Assata*, 49, 50, 52.

Chapter 4. Black Family

1. Joyce Kelly, "Father Absence 'Decimates' Black Community in U.S.," Reuters (June 14, 2007), https://www.reuters.com/article/us-usa-fathers/father-absence-decimates-black-community-in-u-s-idUSN0419185720070614; Obama speech: https://www.politico.com/story/2008/06/text-of-obamas-fatherhood-speech-011094; Cosby speech: https://www.americanrhetoric.com/speeches/billcosbypoundcakespeech.htm.

2. See James T. Patterson, *Freedom Is Not Enough: The Moynihan Report and America's Struggle over Black Family Life from LBJ to Obama* (New York: Basic Books, 2012).

3. But see Jennifer Nash's important work exploring the fetishized figure of the resilient Black mother: *Birthing Black Mothers* (Durham, NC: Duke University Press, 2021).

4. James Baldwin, *Collected Essays* (New York: Library of America, 1998), 7; Ralph Ellison, *Invisible Man* (New York: Vintage, 1995), 345. See also Hortense J. Spillers, "Papa's Baby, Mama's Maybe: An American Grammar Book," *Diacritics* 17, no. 2 (Summer 1987): 64–81.

5. Ellison, *Invisible Man*, 191, 218; James Baldwin, *Notes of a Native Son* (New York: Dial, 1963).

6. Keeanga-Yamahtta Taylor, ed., *How We Get Free: Black Feminism and the Combahee River Collective* (Chicago: Haymarket Books, 2017), 18.

7. Richard Wright, *Native Son* (New York: Harper Perennial, 2005), 64.

8. Richard Wright, *Black Boy* (New York: Harper, 2008), 10, 3, 7.

9. Wright, *Native Son*, 62.

10. Wright, *Native Son*, 241, 235.

11. Baldwin, *Notes of a Native Son.*

12. Baldwin, *Essays,* 253.

13. Baldwin, *Notes of a Native Son,* 78, 80.

14. Baldwin, *Notes of a Native Son,* 78; James Baldwin, *Go Tell It on the Mountain* (New York: Vintage, 2013), 262. Even holiness is not unequivocally beautiful in the novel, as Bill Frucht helpfully pointed out to me. I elaborate on this analysis in "The Negative Political Theology of James Baldwin," in *A Political Companion to James Baldwin,* ed. Susan J. McWilliams (Lexington: University Press of Kentucky, 2017), 171–94.

15. Alice Walker, *The Color Purple* (New York: Harcourt Brace Jovanovich, 1982), 162, 215, 167, 175.

16. Walker, *The Color Purple,* 235, 176.

17. Audre Lorde, *Zami: A New Spelling of My Name* (Watertown, MA: Persephone, 1982).

18. Lorde, *Zami,* 3, 252. Lorde's spelling of "dykes" is a deliberate pun.

19. Lorde, *Zami,* 3, 4. More precisely, Lorde imagines DeLois as undominated, an icon of freedom pointing to the joyous life that will be once the struggle against domination succeeds.

20. Lorde, *Zami,* 203, 209.

21. Lorde, *Zami,* 58.

22. Lorde, *Zami,* 65, 33, 32, 18, 83. Compare Houria Bouteldja, *Whites, Jews, and Us* (South Pasadena, CA: Semiotext(e), 2016), 126, where Bouteldja asserts that dignity is in the "relationship between a mother and her child and in the fluid that allowed the daughter to draw from it an education and learn to look white people in the face."

23. Barack Obama, *Dreams from My Father: A Story of Race and Inheritance* (New York: Crown, 2004).

24. Ta-Nehisi Coates, *Between the World and Me* (New York: Spiegel & Grau, 2015); Coates, *The Beautiful Struggle* (New York: Spiegel & Grau, 2008). This tendency to fit Black coming-of-age narratives into white, patriarchal structures is not solely the domain of men: compare the memoirs of Roxanne Gay, Tracy K. Smith, and Elizabeth Alexander, each longing for something, for a father-like authority, and each eventually sating that longing through some means. I elaborate on this reading of Coates in "Black Futures and Black Fathers," in *Between the World of Ta-Nehisi Coates and Christianity,* ed. David Evans and Peter Dula (Eugene, OR: Cascade Books, 2018), 24–36.

25. Darnell L. Moore, *No Ashes in the Fire: Coming of Age Black & Free in America* (New York: Nation Books, 2018).

26. Patrisse Khan-Cullors and asha bandele, *When They Call You a Terrorist: A Black Lives Matter Memoir* (New York: St. Martin's, 2018).

Chapter 5. Black Futures

1. Aimé Césaire, *Notebook of a Return to a Native Land* (Middletown, CT: Wesleyan University Press, 2001), 22. Thanks to Wesleyan University Press for permission to quote from this poem. While Césaire did become a reformer later in life and was viewed with suspicion by a younger generation of radicals in Martinique, his early poetic and political vision embraced a distinctive revolutionary spirit. See Gary Wilder, *Freedom Time: Negritude, Decolonization, and the Future of the World* (Durham, NC: Duke University Press, 2015). Frantz Fanon discusses Césaire's phrase in *Black Skins, White Masks* (London: Pluto, 2008), 71, 168, and in some scholarship, including Frank Wilderson's, the phrase is at times attributed to Fanon rather than Césaire. For discussion of the phrase's migration and the political and intellectual confusion it creates, see Greg Thomas, "Afro-Blue Notes: The Death of Afro-pessimism (2.0)?" *Theory & Event* 21, no. 1 (January 2018): 282–317.

2. Frank B. Wilderson, III, *Afropessimism* (New York: Liverlight, 2020), 171, 205, 206.

3. Adrienne Marie Brown, *Emergent Strategy: Shaping Change, Changing Worlds* (Chico, CA: AK, 2017); Octavia E. Butler, *Parable of the Sower* (New York: Four Walls Eight Windows, 1983); Butler, *Parable of the Talents* (New York: Open Road Integrated Media, 2012).

4. https://blacklivesmatter.com/black-futures-month/ (accessed June 1, 2020; no longer available). See also Kimberly Drew and Jenna Wortham, eds., *Black Futures* (New York: One World, 2020).

5. Christopher Lasch, *The True and Only Heaven: Progress and Its Critics* (New York: Norton, 1991); Cornel West, *Hope on a Tightrope: Words and Wisdom* (Carlsbad, CA: Smiley, 2008), especially 38; Vincent Lloyd, "For What Are Whites to Hope?" *Political Theology* 17, no. 2 (2016): 168–81.

6. Friedrich Nietzsche, *Untimely Meditations*, trans. R. J. Holingdale (Cambridge: Cambridge University Press, 1997).

7. Reagan's speech: https://www.reaganlibrary.gov/sspeeches/122388c; Martin Luther King, Jr., *A Testament of Hope: The Essential Writings and Speeches of Martin Luther King, Jr.* (San Francisco: HarperSanFrancisco, 1991).

8. Eli Clare, *Brilliant Imperfection: Grappling with Cure* (Durham, NC: Duke University Press, 2017); Elizabeth Barnes, *The Minority Body: A Theory of Disability* (Oxford: Oxford University Press, 2016).

9. Martin Luther King, Jr., "The Meaning of Hope," sermon delivered at Dexter Avenue Baptist Church (December 10, 1967), The King Center Digital Archive, http://www.thekingcenter.org/archive/document/meaning-hope (accessed February

20, 2018; no longer available online, held at King Center Library and Archives). I elaborate on these points in Vincent Lloyd, " 'A Moral Astigmatism': King on Hope and Illusion," *Telos* 182 (Spring 2018): 121–38.

10. King, "The Meaning of Hope."

11. Clayborne Carson, "Martin Luther King, Jr.: Charismatic Leadership in a Mass Struggle," *Journal of American History* 74, no. 2 (September 1987): 448–54; Erica R. Edwards, *Charisma and the Fictions of Black Leadership* (Minneapolis: University of Minnesota Press, 2012). On Delany as part of a Black political tradition, see Alex Zamalin, *Black Utopia: The History of an Idea from Black Nationalism to Afrofuturism* (New York: Columbia University Press, 2019). I elaborate on these thoughts about Delany in Vincent Lloyd, "The Prophet Samuel R. Delany," in *Prophecy in a Secular Age*, ed. David True (Eugene, OR: Cascade Books, 2020), 90–108.

12. Samuel R. Delany, *Heavenly Breakfast: An Essay on the Winter of Love* (Flint, MI: Bamberger Books, 1997).

13. Delany, *Heavenly Breakfast*, 15. See also John McDowell, "Virtue and Reason," *Monist* 62, no. 3 (July 1979): 331–50.

14. Delany, *Heavenly Breakfast*, 20.

15. Samuel R. Delany, *The Motion of Light in Water: Sex and Science Fiction Writing in the East Village* (Minneapolis: University of Minnesota Press, 2004), 293; Joan Scott, "The Evidence of Experience," *Critical Inquiry* 17 (1991): 773–97; Delany, *Dhalgren* (New York: Bantam Books, 1975).

16. Samuel R. Delany, *Times Square Red, Times Square Blue* (New York: New York University Press, 1999), xvii–xviii.

17. Delany, *Times Square Red, Times Square Blue*, 15, 40.

18. Delany, *Heavenly Breakfast*, 20.

19. Michael Walzer, *Interpretation and Social Criticism* (Cambridge, MA: Harvard University Press, 1993); George Shulman, *American Prophecy: Race and Redemption in American Political Culture* (Minneapolis: University of Minnesota Press, 2008).

20. Barbara Ransby, "Ella Taught Me: Shattering the Myth of the Leaderless Movement," *Colorlines* (June 12, 2015), https://www.colorlines.com/articles/ella-taught-me-shattering-myth-leaderless-movement.

Chapter 6. Black Magic

1. Patrisse Cullors and Robert Ross, "The Spiritual Work of Black Lives Matter," *On Being* (February 18, 2016), https://onbeing.org/programs/patrisse-cullors-and-robert-ross-the-spiritual-work-of-black-lives-matter-may2017/.

2. See Hebah H. Farrag, "The Role of Spirit in the #BlackLivesMatter Movement," *Religion Dispatches* (June 24, 2015), https://religiondispatches.org/the-role-of-spirit-in-the-blacklivesmatter-movement-a-conversation-with-activist-and-artist-patrisse-cullors/.

3. Essence Harden, "On *Respite, Reprieve, and Healing,*" *Curate L.A.* (May 14, 2019), https://medium.com/@curate.LA/on-respite-reprieve-and-healing-adf968c81080.

4. Biko Gray, "Religion in/and Black Lives Matter: Celebrating the Impossible," *Religion Compass* 13, no. 1 (January 2019); Farrag, "The Role of Spirit in the #BlackLivesMatter Movement."

5. See Jonathon Kahn and Vincent W. Lloyd, eds., *Race and Secularism in America* (New York: Columbia University Press, 2016); Jeffrey Stout, "Religion Unbound: Ideals and Powers from Cicero to King," The Gifford Lectures (2017), https://www.giffordlectures.org/lectures/religion-unbound-ideals-and-powers-cicero-king.

6. Aimé Césaire, *Notebook of a Return to a Native Land* (Middletown, CT: Wesleyan University Press, 2001), 5. Thanks to Wesleyan University Press for permission to quote from Césaire's poem.

7. Césaire, *Notebook,* 7, 8.

8. Césaire, *Notebook,* 9, 6.

9. Césaire, *Notebook,* 17–18.

10. Césaire, *Notebook,* 19, 20.

11. Césaire, *Notebook,* 35, 39.

12. Jesse James DeConto, "Activist Who Took Down Confederate Flag from Statehouse Drew on Faith, Civil Rights Awakening," *Christian Century* (July 14, 2015), https://www.christiancentury.org/article/2015–07/activist-who-took-down-confederate-flag-drew-her-faith-new-civil-rights-awakening; Almeda M. Wright, *The Spiritual Lives of Young African Americans* (New York: Oxford University Press, 2017), 160–61.

13. Sarah van Gelder, "Rev. Sekou on Today's Civil Rights Leaders," *Yes! Magazine* (July 22, 2015), https://www.yesmagazine.org/social-justice/2015/07/22/black-lives-matter-s-favorite-minister-reverend-sekou-young-queer/; Rev. Sekou & the Holy Ghost, "The Revolution Has Come" (January 31, 2016), https://www.youtube.com/watch?v=6P3zsqllb2A; Jake Dockter, "The Gospel Is Not a Netural Term: An Interview with Rev. Sekou" (October 24, 2014), https://medium.com/theology-of-ferguson/the-gospel-is-not-a-neutral-term-an-interview-with-rev-sekou-ae7990e66fe2.

14. W. E. B. Du Bois, *Du Bois on Religion,* ed. Phil Zuckerman (Walnut Creek, CA: AltaMira, 2000); James Cone, *The Cross and the Lynching Tree* (Maryknoll, NY: Orbis Books, 2011); Kelly Brown Douglas, *Stand Your Ground: Black Bodies and the*

Justice of God (New York: Orbis Books, 2015); James Cone, *Speaking the Truth: Ecumenism, Liberation, and Black Theology* (Grand Rapids, MI: Eerdmans, 1986), 20.

15. Denys Turner, "Marxism, Liberation Theology, and the Way of Negation," in *The Cambridge Companion to Liberation Theology*, ed. Christopher Rowland (Cambridge: Cambridge University Press, 1999), 199–217; Ashon Crawley, *Blackpentecostal Breath: The Aesthetics of Possibility* (New York: Fordham University Press, 2017).

16. James H. Cone, *Martin & Malcolm & America: A Dream or a Nightmare* (Maryknoll, NY: Orbis Books, 1991), 165.

17. Vincent W. Lloyd, *Religion of the Field Negro: On Black Secularism and Black Theology* (New York: Fordham University Press, 2017); Alistair Kee, *The Rise and Demise of Black Liberation Theology* (London: SCM, 2008); Ivan Petrella, *The Future of Liberation Theology: An Argument and Manifesto* (London: Routledge, 2016); Delores S. Williams, *Sisters in the Wilderness: The Challenge of Womanist God-Talk* (Maryknoll, NY: Orbis Books, 1993).

18. Ruth Wilson Gilmore, *Golden Gulag: Prisons, Surplus, Crisis, and Opposition in Globalizing California* (Berkeley: University of California Press, 2007), 28; Abdul R. JanMohamed, *The Death-Bound-Subject: Richard Wright's Archaeology of Death* (Durham, NC: Duke University Press, 2005).

19. Cullors and Ross, "The Spiritual Work of Black Lives Matter." See also Brandon M. Terry and Judith Butler, "The Radical Equality of Lives," *Boston Review* (January 7, 2020), http://bostonreview.net/philosophy-religion/brandon-m-terry-judith-butler-radical-equality-lives.

20. Brooke Obie, "For Activist Rev. Sekou, 'The Revolution Has Come,' " *Ebony* (February 10, 2016), https://www.ebony.com/news/rev-sekou-interview/. See also Alain Badiou, *Saint Paul: The Foundation of Universalism* (Stanford, CA: Stanford University Press, 2003).

21. Cone, *Speaking the Truth*, 34; Cone, *A Black Theology of Liberation* (Maryknoll, NY: Orbis Books, 1986), 136; Cone, *Risks of Faith: The Emergence of a Black Theology of Liberation, 1968–1998* (Boston: Beacon, 1999), 7.

22. Césaire, *Notebook*, 14, 16, 20, 51.

23. Césaire, *Notebook*, 2. See also Simone Weil, *Gravity and Grace* (New York: Putnam, 1952).

Chapter 7. I Believe in the Revolution

1. Advance the Struggle, "Justice for Oscar Grant: A Lost Opportunity?" (2009), https://advancethestruggle.wordpress.com/2009/07/15/justice-for-oscar-grant-a-lost-opportunity/.

2. Lynice Pinkard, "The Master's Mehserle Can Never Dismantle the Master's House," *Tikkun* 26, no. 1 (Winter 2011): 89.

3. Lynice Pinkard, "Revolutionary Suicide: Risking Everything to Transform Society and Live Fully," *Tikkun* 28, no. 4 (Fall 2013): 31–41. See also Huey P. Newton, *Revolutionary Suicide* (New York: Harcourt Brace Jovanovich, 1973).

4. Pinkard, "Revolutionary Suicide," 41; Wesley Lowery, *They Can't Kill Us All: Ferguson, Baltimore, and the New Era in America's Racial Justice Movement* (New York: Little, Brown, 2016), 87. Punctuation and capitalization in Garza's Facebook post have been regularized.

5. Angela Davis, *Abolition Democracy: Beyond Empire, Prisons, and Torture* (New York: Seven Stories, 2005); Davis, *Are Prisons Obsolete?* (New York: Seven Stories, 2003).

6. Mariame Kaba, *We Do This 'til We Free Us: Abolitionist Organizing and Transforming Justice* (Chicago: Haymarket Books, 2021); Ruth Wilson Gilmore, *Change Everything: Racial Capitalism and the Case for Abolition* (Chicago: Haymarket, 2022).

7. Lisa Guenther, "These Are the Moments in Which Another World Becomes Possible," *Abolition Journal* (July 10, 2015), https://abolitionjournal.org/lisa-guenther-abolition-statement/.

8. Advance the Struggle, "Justice for Oscar Grant."

9. Advance the Struggle, "Justice for Oscar Grant." See also *The Revolution Will Not Be Funded: Beyond the Non-Profit Industrial Complex*, ed. INCITE! (Durham, NC: Duke University Press, 2017).

10. See the "Principles of Unity" of Advance the Struggle's sister organization, Unity and Struggle: http://www.unityandstruggle.org/about/principles-of-unity/. Democratic Socialists of America, which saw a membership boom in the 2010s, generally fits this description but has a broader ideological tent and a looser sense of organizational discipline than revolutionary socialist organizations.

11. C. L. R. James, *The Black Jacobins: Toussaint L'Ouverture and the San Domingo Revolution* (New York: Dial, 1938); Paul Buhle, *C. L. R. James: The Artist as Revolutionary* (New York: Verso, 1988); Grace Lee Boggs, *Living for Change: An Autobiography* (Minneapolis: University of Minnesota Press, 1998); C. L. R. James, unpublished autobiography, C. L. R. James Papers, Rare Book and Manuscript Library, Columbia University, New York. I expand on these ideas in Vincent Lloyd, "The Puritan Atheism of C. L. R. James," in *Beyond Man: Race, Coloniality, and Philosophy of Religion*, ed. An Yountae and Eleanor Craig (Durham, NC: Duke University Press, 2021), 108–26.

12. C. L. R. James and Grace C. Lee, *Facing Reality* (Detroit: Bewick, 1974), 7.

13. James and Lee, *Facing Reality*, chap. 7.

14. James and Lee, *Facing Reality*, 75. See also James Boggs, *Pages from a Black Radical's Notebook: A James Boggs Reader*, ed. Stephen M. Ward (Detroit: Wayne State University Press, 2011); Grace Lee Boggs, *The Next American Revolution: Sustainable Activism for the Twenty-First Century* (Berkeley: University of California Press, 2011).

15. James and Lee, *Facing Reality*, 94.

16. James and Lee, *Facing Reality*, 99.

17. See Hal Draper, *Socialism from Below* (Atlantic Highlands, NJ: Humanities, 1992).

18. James and Lee, *Facing Reality*, 165; James, unpublished autobiography. See also W. Chris Johnson, "Sex and the Subversive Alien: The Moral Life of C. L. R. James," *International Journal of Francophone Studies* 14, nos. 1–2 (2011): 185–203; Lloyd, "Puritan Atheism of C. L. R. James."

19. See C. L. R. James, *Beyond a Boundary* (Durham, NC: Duke University Press, 2013). For an assessment of the tragic in James's work, see David Scott, *Conscripts of Modernity: The Tragedy of Colonial Enlightenment* (Durham, NC: Duke University Press, 2004). The epistemic privilege of the oppressed may seem counterintuitive since those most dominated would seem most helpless. However, those most dominated are primed for struggle because the mismatch between ideology and reality is most evident in their lives and on their bodies. Some of these issues are explored further in José Medina, *The Epistemology of Resistance: Gender and Racial Oppression, Epistemic Injustice and Resistant Imaginations* (New York: Oxford University Press, 2013).

20. For arguments along related lines, see Adolph Reed, " 'What Are the Drums Saying, Booker?' The Current Crisis of the Black Intellectual," *Village Voice* (April 11, 1995), 31–36; Sara Ahmed, *On Being Included: Racism and Diversity in Institutional Life* (Durham, NC: Duke University Press, 2012).

21. Robin D. G. Kelley, "Black Study, Black Struggle," *Boston Review* (March 7, 2016), http://bostonreview.net/forum/robin-d-g-kelley-black-study-black-struggle.

22. This does not necessarily mean excluding academics, but rather questioning whether it is necessary for them to enter political activity *as* academics, or "scholar-activists."

23. Friedrich Nietzsche, *On the Genealogy of Morality* (Cambridge: Cambridge University Press, 1994). See also Wendy Brown, *States of Injury: Power and Freedom in Late Modernity* (Princeton, NJ: Princeton University Press, 1995).

24. Nietzsche, *On the Genealogy of Morality*, 28.

25. See Giorgio Agamben, *The Signature of All Things: On Method* (New York: Zone Books, 2009).

26. Sylvia Wynter, "Unsettling the Coloniality of Being/Power/Truth/Freedom: Towards the Human, After Man, Its Overrepresentation—an Argument," *CR: The New Centennial Review* 3, no. 3 (Fall 2003): 312.

Afterword

1. This framing of ethics is structurally similar to that found in the work of Alain Badiou (with domination replacing the revolutionary event as the occupant of the ontological register). See, for example, Badiou, *Ethics: An Essay on Understanding of Evil* (London: Verso, 2001); Badiou, *Saint Paul: The Foundation of Universalism* (Stanford, CA: Stanford University Press, 2003). There are also strong resonances with the concept of *jihad*, struggle, in Islamic thought and practice; on the ambivalences of this term, see Michael Bonner, *Jihad in Islamic Thought* (Princeton, NJ: Princeton University Press, 2006). See also Maytha Alhassen and Ahmed Shihab-Eldin, eds., *Demanding Dignity: Young Voices from the Front Lines of the Arab Revolutions* (Ashland, OR: White Cloud, 2012). Bill Frucht helpfully suggests resonances with the concept of *satori* in Zen Buddhism as well. Of course, the foundational nature of struggle is at the heart of the Christian tradition, in Augustine's *Confessions*.

2. This sense of ascetic practices as resistance to ideology is developed by Michel Foucault and helpfully applied to contemporary conditions by Elettra Stimilli in her book *Debt of the Living: Ascesis and Capitalism* (Albany: State University of New York Press, 2017).

3. Louis Althusser, "Ideology and Ideological State Apparatuses," in *Lenin and Philosophy and Other Essays* (New York: Monthly Review, 2001), 85–125.

4. Sylvia Wynter, "Unsettling the Coloniality of Being/Power/Truth/Freedom: Towards the Human, After Man, Its Overrepresentation—an Argument," *CR: The New Centennial Review* 3, no. 3 (Fall 2003): 257–337. See also Bonnie Honig's discussion of contemporary humanisms in the first part of her *Antigone, Interrupted* (Cambridge: Cambridge University Press, 2013).

5. Robyn Wiegman and Elizabeth A. Wilson, eds., "Queer Theory without Antinormativity," special issue of *differences* 26, no. 1 (May 2015); Janet R. Jakobsen, "Queer Is? Queer Does? Normativity and the Problem of Resistance," *GLQ* 4, no. 4 (1998): 511–36.

6. Lisa Tessman, *Burdened Virtues: Virtue Ethics for Liberatory Struggles* (New York: Oxford University Press, 2005); Simone Weil, *Gravity and Grace* (New York: Putnam, 1952). See also Amia Srinivasan, "The Aptness of Anger," *Journal of Political Philosophy* 26, no. 2 (June 2018): 123–44.

7. Group labels may serve as shorthand for collectives in action, and I use them this way at times. On epistemic privilege, see José Medina, *The Epistemology of Resistance: Gender and Racial Oppression, Epistemic Injustice and Resistant Imaginations* (New York: Oxford University Press, 2013).

Acknowledgments

I was fortunate to be able to share material from this book at a number of lectures and workshops where I received helpful feedback. Special thanks are due to Frank Wilderson and Roberto Sirvent for inviting me to the University of California, Irvine; to Charles Mathewes and Paul Jones for inviting me to University of Virginia; and to Jennifer Herdt and Kathy Chow for inviting me to Yale. I am grateful to the Louisville Institute and Villanova University for funding the sabbatical during which I researched this book, to Saint Louis University for providing me an institutional affiliation, and to David Meconi, SJ, for providing me an office. An Alan Richardson Fellowship at Durham University brought me to a beautiful town in which to think and write, and conversations with Karen Kilby there were invaluable. I am grateful to my research assistants Laura Simpson and Rahma Goran. Mark Shiffman and Siddhant Issar offered helpful comments on the whole manuscript. I was not able to adequately respond to valuable feedback from Alys Weinbaum, but it helped launch my next book project. Sharmila Sen sharpened my prose and helped me understand the sort of book I did not want to write. Copyeditor Robin DuBlanc did a wonderful job. My editor Bill Frucht stands in a class of his own as a careful reader and thinker who pushed me in just the right places.

Index

abolitionism: abolition of slavery, 164; abolitionists compared to revolutionaries, 136–37, 139; political stance, 159–60; prison abolitionism, 20, 22, 135–37

accountability: Black studies, 29; Christian, 123; of philosophy, 32, 34, 36, 37, 99

Achilles, 42

Advance the Struggle, 138–40, 144

Aeschylus, 42

Afropessimism, 24–27, 31, 94–95

Ahmed, Sara, 51

Alinsky, Saul, 138

allegory of the cave, 31–32, 149

Althusser, Louis, 156, 158

Athena, 42

Augustine, 64, 179n1

Axelrod, Beverly, 70

Badiou, Alain, 179n1

Baldwin, James, 18, 77, 78–79, 82–85, 110

Barry, Dante, 57

Beatles, 59, 70

Beyoncé, 22

Biden, Joseph, 5

Black Alliance for Just Immigration, 21

Black girl magic, 132

Black joy, 33. *See also* joy

Black Lives Matter movement, 5, 93

Black Panther Party, 18, 56, 72, 139

Black power movement: account of love in, 56, 58, 66; and Black liberation theology, 125; and Black studies, 29; dignity in, 1; eclipsing civil rights discourse, 21; King on, 45

Black studies, 29–31, 146–47

Black Youth Project 100, 57

Boggs, Grace Lee, 140

Bouteldja, Houria, 5, 172n22

Brown, Adrienne Marie, 95–96

Brown, Austin Channing, 52

Brown, Autumn, 95

Brown, Michael, vii, 39, 49, 123

Butler, Octavia, 49, 95–96, 104

Carmichael, Stokley, 1, 21, 46, 105

Carruthers, Charlene, 57, 62

Césaire, Aimé, xiii, 94, 96, 118–22, 128–29

Christianity: and Black Lives Matter, 93, 112, 113, 118, 122; and death, 127–28; and domination, 123–25; Douglass on, 8; feminist, 126; hope in, 97; image of God, 117; Malcolm X on, 56, 125; King on, 58, 103, 104,

Christianity (*continued*)
125; love in, 64; Obama on, 91;
Sekou on 123; whiteness of, 115, 118.
See also God; Jesus; liberation
theology
Cleaver, Eldridge, 65, 66–70, 72
Coates, Ta-Nehisi, 49, 91
Combahee River Collective, 79–80
Communism, 80
Cone, James, 118, 124, 125, 127–28
Cooper, Brittney, 53–55
Cosby, Bill, 74, 83
Cose, Ellis, 48
Covey, Edward, 6–7, 9, 10–11, 13, 164
Crawley, Ashon, 125
crucifixion, 103, 133
Cullors, Patrisse, 1, 21, 56–57, 63, 92,
112–14, 127

D Smoke, 22, 113
dance: Césaire on, 121, 122; Hughes
on, 4, 5; titillating, 33
Davis, Angela, 1, 47, 136
Davis, Ossie, 3
death: Césaire on, 128–29; Cone on,
127–28; Douglass on, 8, 9; fear of, 8;
social, 27; vulnerability to, 126–28,
133
Delany, Samuel R., 104–11
Dellums, Ron, 131
Democratic Party, 19
Democratic Socialists of America,
177n10
dignitaries, 16
Dignity and Power Now, 1, 112
disability, 101
Douglas, Kelly Brown, 124
Douglass, Frederick, 6–11, 13,
163–64
Dunayevskaya, Raya, 140

Ellison, Ralph, xii, 62–63, 77, 78, 86
end of the world. *See* world, end of the
environment: natural, 129; racism and,
39, 126
epistemology: epistemic privilege,
178n19; ontology and, 153, 162
equality: Douglass aspires for, 7;
hypocrisy about, 26; relationship
with dignity, 16–17
Eumenides, 42
excellence, Black, 118

faith, 133–34; Newsome's, 122; in
tradition, 152. *See also* Christianity;
spirituality
Farrakhan, Louis, 47
Ferguson, Missouri, vii–viii, xi, xii, 39,
53, 123
flourishing: accompanying struggle,
33, 127, 155, 158–59; Black life, 127;
eschatological, 93–94, 101; fugitivity
as, 26; privilege blocking, 33;
sociality as, 27
Floyd, George, xii–xiii, 20, 33, 76
Ford, Ezell, 113
freedom: Christian, 119; dreaming of,
11, 103; on eschatological horizon,
64, 69; experiments in, 105–9; false
promises of, 19, 141; and hope, 103;
hypocrisy about, 26; inward
struggle for, 131–32; Lorde's
depiction of, 172n19; love directed
toward, 61, 63, 66, 69, 98; Shakur
on, 73; struggle as foretaste of, 7, 8,
123, 127–29, 161
fugitivity, 26–27, 31, 147, 152

Garvey, Marcus, 1
Garza, Alicia, 1, 21, 56–57, 73, 96,
134

Gilmore, Ruth Wilson, 126
Giuliani, Rudolph, 108
God: anchoring normativity, 78;
    Baldwin on, 83–85; in Black Lives
    Matter organizing, 112, 114, 122–24;
    Césaire on, 121; in *The Color Purple*,
    70–71, 86–87; Cone on, 125; Garza
    on, 57; image of, 2, 117; killing, 121;
    liberation theology's account of,
    116–17, 124–26; little gods, 59;
    mastery, 41, 78–79, 114–15; in *Native
    Son*, 81; negative theology, 124;
    Obama on, 91; in *Zami*, 88. *See also*
    Jesus
Grant, Oscar, 131–32, 138, 144
Gray, Biko, 114
Guenther, Lisa, 137

Hacker, Marilyn, 105
Haiti, 6, 140, 146
healing, 22, 96, 106, 112–13, 114
Hegel, G. W. F., 32
Hill, Joe, 137
Hill, Lauryn, 39–41
Holocaust, Jewish, 35, 168n28
Homer, 42
homosexuality. *See* queerness
honor, 16
hooks, bell, 47–48, 49
hope: Afropessimism's refusal of,
    26, 94; in Black Lives Matter, 93;
    in civil rights movement, 93;
    cure as object of, 100–101;
    domination contaminating, 97,
    101; King on, 99–100, 102–4, 111;
    mother as figure of, 76; in
    multiculturalism, 48; versus
    optimism, 97
Hughes, Langston, 4, 5
Hungarian revolution, 141–42

identity politics, 19, 107
ideology, 28–29, 156, 178n19, 179n2
idolatry, 59, 82, 86, 121, 124
Ifá, 113, 114
Iliad, 42
imagination, 10, 96, 111; and dignity,
    5–6; Douglass's, 164; organizers
    amplifying, 144; and philosophy,
    152; struggle and, 9–10; Wilderson
    on, 95
incarceration. *See* prisons
indignation, 40, 45, 48, 92, 119
intellectuals, Black, 146–47. *See also*
    Black studies

Jackson, George, 65, 66–67, 68–70,
    73
Jackson, Phillip, 74
James, C. L. R., 32, 140–46
Jehovah's Witnesses, 92
Jesus: in Black Lives Matter, 112,
    122, 123, 127; commitment to
    struggle, 103; Cone on, 128;
    image of God, 124; King on,
    72, 103; love, 72; symbol of
    domination, 123, 124. *See also*
    Christianity; God
Johnson-Forest Tendency, 140–46
joy, 33, 78, 172n19; love and, 71
Judges, dignity of, 4, 8, 16
judgment: avoiding, 19, 28, 29, 70–71;
    domination distorts, 65; form of
    struggle, 37; guided by ideal types,
    66; improved by struggle, 54; love
    requires, 72; and privilege, 161; and
    rhetoric, 163
justice: Cone on, 125; left's commit-
    ment to, 20; love and, 60, 85;
    meaning of, 6, 20; beyond public
    policy, 20

"Karens", 54
Katrina (hurricane), 49, 74
Kelley, Robin, 147–48
Key, Keegan-Michael, 49
King, Jr., Martin Luther: account of
  hope, 93, 97, 99, 102–4; account of
  love, 56, 58–61, 72; assassination of,
  105; in cultural memory, vii, 57, 58;
  eclipsed by Black Power, 21, 66;
  holiday, 99; indignation of, 45–46;
  invoking dignity, 1, 9; Malcolm X
  and, 56, 125; memorial, 93; as
  prophet, 110; on white liberals,
  63–64
King, Rodney, 26, 39

leadership: in Black Lives Matter, 110,
  134; James as, 145; King as, 99, 104;
  religious, 102, 149; of vanguard, 142;
  working class, 143
left: Black dignity as vision for, 20;
  versus liberal, 19, 135–36
Levinas, Emmanuel, 35–36
liberalism: versus leftists, 19, 135–36;
  and nonprofits 139; Obama as
  liberal, 97; political philosophy, 19;
  white liberals, 33, 46, 63–64, 75,
  81, 91
liberation theology, 116–17, 118,
  122–26. See also Christianity; Cone,
  James.
Lorde, Audre: on Shakur, 73; "Uses of
  Anger," 49–51, 52, 53; "Uses of the
  Erotic," 71–72; Zami, xii, 87–90
Lugones, María, 51–52

madness: Baldwin on, 84–85; Césaire
  on, 120–21; Hill on, 40; and rage,
  44
Malcolm X, 1, 46, 56, 58, 125

Martin, Trayvon, 20, 21, 38–39, 49
Million Hoodies for Justice, 57
modernity: effect on dignity, 16,
  normativity in, 28, 29, requiring
  anti-Blackness, 25, 26–27
Montgomery bus boycott, 9, 60
Moore, Darnell, 53, 92
moralizing, 33–34, 75, 123, 129
Morrison, Toni, 18
Moten, Fred, 26
mourning, 127, 137
Movement for Black Lives platform,
  1, 21
Moynihan, Daniel Patrick, 75
Muhammad, Elijah, 83
multiculturalism: in academia, 30, 31;
  Afropessimism's rejection of, 26;
  avoiding normativity, 19, 29; Black
  family and, 74, 75; Black liberation
  theology and, 125; Coates and, 91;
  Delany and, 107; end of, 20–21, 24,
  38–39, 49, 91; and hooks, 47–48;
  language of Black politics, viii;
  managing love, 56, 58; managing
  memory of King, 46, 58; muting
  justice claims, 18–20, 23; patriarchy
  and, 90; practices of, x, 18; Walker
  and, 71
mutual aid, 106, 166n11

negative theology, 124
Negritude, 118, 121
Newsome, Bree, 122
Newton, Huey P., 132
Nietzsche, Friedrich, 28, 98, 149–50
nonprofits, 33, 138, 139, 140, 144
normativity, 28–29, 157–58

Obama, Barack: anger of, 48;
  invoking dignity, 1; on fathers, 74,

83, 90–91; on hope, 97; organizer, 138; reflections on Trayvon Martin, 38; respectability, 5; symbol of multiculturalism, 18, 21

Obama, Michelle, 53

Occupy Wall Street, 19, 39, 135

ontic, 10–15, 153–62, 166n14

ontological, 10–15, 35, 152, 153–62, 179n1

organizing: accountability to, 34, 36; and Beyoncé, 22; and Black studies, 29, 31; and dignity, 3, 9, and intellectuals, 146, 147, 149; effects of, 24; Johnson-Forest on, 143–44; and love, 61; and philosophy, 32; political significance of, 137–40; rage channeled in, 51, 53; and struggle, 17

Palin, Sarah, 97

patriarchy: and Black girl magic, 118; condemned in Movement for Black Lives platform, 22; and family, 78, 83, 86; and King's charisma, 104; Lorde's challenge to, 90; marked by rape, 14, 15; quieting women's rage, 44; Sanders on, 135; Walker's challenge to, 90

peace, 45, 105, 113–14

Pentecostalism, 125

performance: Cooper on, 53; dignity as, 2, 5, 8–10, 41; excellence as, 118; fugitive, 147; and rage, 45, 53; Robeson's, 3

philosophy, 22–24; academic, 22, 31, 148; accountable to social movements, 32; Black, 14, 32; Black habits as, 22; and domination, 149–50; European, ix, 32; James on, 32; King on, 59; Levinas on, 35; and love, 60; norms for, 152, 162–63;

routed through slavery, 36; simulacra, 152; as way of life, 164

Pinkard, Lynice, 18, 131–33, 138

Plato, 31, 32, 149–50

prisons: abolition of, 20, 135–37, 160; carceral feminism, 148; and philosophy, 31, 149; and slavery, 67

prophet: in Black Lives Matter, 110; Césaire on, 121; Delany as, 110–11; King as, 58, 102, 110–11; Walzer on, 110

queerness: curing, 100–101; imagining family, 75; queer theory, 157–58

racial capitalism, 167n21

rape, xii, 14, 15, 40, 73, 153

Reagan, Ronald, 99

recognition, desire for, 10–11

Redmond, Shana, 3

reformism, 26, 96, 131, 136–37, 160

relationality, 28, 77

reparations, 20

respectability, 5, 49, 54–55

resurrection, 8, 82, 123, 131

revolution: from below, 134–35; Black power and, 56, 67; Cleaver on, 70; compared to abolition, 136–37, 139; dignity entailing, 134; Jackson on, 69–70; and love, 57; Pinkard on, 132–33; Sanders on, 135; Sekou on, 123, 127; Shakur as, 72–73. *See also* Haiti; Hungarian revolution; Johnson-Forest tendency

Revolutionary Communist Party (RCP), 138–39

Robeson, Paul, 2–4

Sanders, Bernie, 135

Schmitt, Carl, 166n13

Scott, Joan, 107

Scottsboro Boys, 4, 8

secularism: ideology of, 115; King's hope secularized, 97

Sekou, Osagyefo Uhuru, 123, 127

self-determination: Black Lives Matter demand, 22; capacity for, 140, 146; and fatherhood, 76; and healing, 113, 114; hooks on, 47; Sekou on, 123

Sexton, Jared, 26

Shakur, Assata, 49, 72–73

Shulman, George, 110

slavery: and Afropessimism, 25–26; afterlives, 12, 21, 25, 75; ambiguity of, 17, 60; Césaire on, 128–29; desire to escape master, xii; Douglass on, 6–9, 11, 163–64; and hope, 98–99; as ideal type, 151; and intellectuals, 146–47; King on, 103; and love, 61–64; Nietzsche on, 149–50; paradigm of domination, 10, 14; and philosophy, 36; primal scene, xi, xii, 12, 13, 14; and rage, 40–41; and Robeson, 3; slave catchers, 147; and spirituality, 114–16; struggle of enslaved, 10; vulnerability to death in, 127

Smith, Mychal Denzel, 46, 49

social media, 21, 24, 57, 136

socialism, 19, 82, 138–42

spirituality: ascribed to Blacks, 100; and Black Lives Matter, 112–15, 126; Césaire on, 118–22, 128; and death, 127–28; and environment, 129; Lorde on, 88, 89; and struggle, 115–18, 130; Walker on, 70, 86

status, dignity as, 2–5, 9, 16, 35, 55, 77

Student Nonviolent Coordinating Committee, 56

Summer of Love, 59, 105

survival: anger channeled for, 50–51; Brown sisters on, 95; Cooper on, 54; Cullers on, 92; form of Black life, 127; healing necessary for, 112–13; struggle for, 3, 162

Terrell, Mary Church, 54, 55, 79

Tessman, Lisa, 158

theology. See Christianity; God; spirituality

Thomas, Bigger, xii, 80–83, 86

Till, Emmett, 67

Tillich, Paul, 60

Tippett, Krista, 112

Tometi, Opal, 1, 21, 57

tradition, 150–52

tragedy: James on, 178n19; tragic nature of world, x, 88, 102, 163; tragic situation of intellectuals, 145–46

Tubman, Harriet, 79–80

tyrant, as figure of domination, 7, 8

United Nations: embracing dignity in Charter, 16; petitioned by Paul Robeson, 2

Unity and Struggle, 177n10

Universal Declaration of Human Rights, 16

university, 29–30, 147–49. See also Black studies

Waldron, Jeremy, 16

Walker, Alice, 70–72, 86–87, 88, 90

Walzer, Michael, 110

Washington, Harold, 91

Webb, Constance, 145

West, Kanye, 49

Wilderson, Frank, 26, 94–95, 173n1